EMOTIONAL

INTELLIGENCE

A Practical Guide to Making Friends with Your Emotions and Raising Your EQ

ILONA WRIGHT

DISCLAIMER

TABLE OF CONTENT

INTRODUCTION

The quest to understand emotions dates back to ancient times when philosophers like Aristotle, the Greek philosopher, placed forth their own ideas on the essence and function of emotions. Aristotle argued that desires represented an essential part of moral perfection. American scholar and educator William James has a clear perspective on feeling. He proposed that feelings were the result of different hormonal shifts being undergone by the human body in response to the external world.

In the timeframe between Aristotle's time and today, psychologists and scientists have promoted many hypotheses that have sought to understand where emotions come from, and why they matter. Robert Plutchik, a professor and researcher, has conceptualized one of the most common hypotheses. Plutchik came up with a wheel of emotions (known as Plutchik's wheel of emotions) which shows that all other emotions come from eight primary emotions. In this circle are balanced against each other opposing emotions. Joy is contrasted with grief, for example, while suspense is juxtaposed with disappointment. In Plutchik's wheel of emotions, the eight core emotions are the happy emotions of love, confidence, anticipation, and disappointment, and the less common emotions of disgust, anxiety, sorrow, and rage.

Why are some people more emotional than others?

If people experience the same kind of feelings, then why do some people seem more intense than others? People who are extremely emotional or extremely responsive are quick to identify. Whereas anyone else appears to be fleetingly absorbing knowledge and feelings, some people wallow longer with their feelings than is often convenient. During tragic movie scenes, they can weep their hearts out, open their homes to abandoned animals, or become easily annoyed by the stuff people do or say, but there was no purpose to offend. At the end, when it comes to their acts and feelings, it's easy to think about an extremely emotional person as being unnecessarily dramatic. The fact of the matter is that this is not a plea for help but a natural response dependent on the wiriness of their brains.

Studying feelings is nowhere near being studied in complete. Scientists are only in the very recent stages of studying feelings, and how they are affected by the genetic structure of humans. As such, it will be a while before there is some agreement about such issues such as extremely vulnerable individuals, and so on. That said, studies have shown that how a person responds to his or her environment is a function of some type of genetic conditioning.

Researcher Rachael Grazioplene and her collaborators performed one such analysis in 2012, and subsequently reported it in The Field of Child Development and Psychiatry. Grazioplene and her colleagues focused on the cholinergic function when conducting this study. The cholinergic mechanism is the body function that controls the kind of interest that we pay to the ambient world and how we interpret the input that we receive from certain conditions. The findings of this study revealed that a specific form of receptor gene referred to as CHRNA4 (from the cholinergic system) will affect how one turns out emotionally based on the type of nutrition this individual gets. As such, the relationship of this gene with the world is a significant determinant of how an infant grows out. The gene CHRNA4 is also named the risk gene or the alert gene.

Think about it: If you've grown up in a family where feelings are nothing to be embarrassed of, you'll most definitely grow up to believe and do the same. If you've grown up loving your parents and family, there are strong odds that you're an adult you'll still be really affectionate towards other individuals. You may be born with the responsive gene as well, but as long as your climate does not allow it to thrive, your emotions will remain repressed. In comparison, a person born with the responsive gene and raised in a highly loving atmosphere would have no trouble being extremely expressive of emotion.

Around the same time it is necessary to remember that regardless of what their society wants them to be, certain individuals will feel the need to behave emotionally.

What is Emotional Intelligence?

Emotional intelligence is a person's ability to identify his or her own emotions and the emotions of those around him or her, to discern the difference between different feelings, and to correctly identify each other, to use emotional information to guide one's own thoughts and actions, to adjust one's emotions to the immediate environment and to regulate emotions. The word has been around since the 1960s but it wasn't until 1995 that the idea was formulated by author Daniel Goleman. Emotional intelligence (EI) is also sometimes referred to as an emotional quotient (EQ), since scholars like to equate it with general (classical) intelligence (IQ). Continuously, research indicate that people with high emotional intelligence excel in all aspects of life; they tend to have improved mental wellbeing, have excellent communication skills, do well in their jobs (especially in places where a lot of interpersonal contact is needed), and they tend to have stronger connections.

Extremely important is emotional intelligence: possessing high emotional intelligence is like understanding what makes people tick. People who are emotionally intelligent realize why they act the way they do, what their own emotional vulnerabilities are, and how they should regulate and manipulate their feelings to achieve what they want; in other terms, people who are emotionally intelligent are the ones who dominate. Empathy is fundamental to emotional intelligence. The term empathy refers to the ability of a person to connect with their own experiences, to understand how others feel. In the modern world our progress relies more frequently than not on our willingness to consider others. So, apart from mastering oneself, emotionally intelligent individuals have another advantage in life: the ability to connect more deeply with others. This illustrates where they will most likely succeed in nearly all areas of life.

There are many different emotional intelligence measurement methods; some are highly technical, and some are fairly straight forward. The Daniel Goleman Method is the most common technique because it was developed by the same individual who invented the concept of emotional intelligence (as we now understand it), and it is quite easy to understand. An emotionally intelligent person, in Goleman's model, should rate highly for the following qualities:

Self-consciousness; which is the ability to understand your own emotions and the strengths and weaknesses.

The capacity to regulate and manage the "disruptive" impulses and behavioral patterns, and the capacity to respond to a shifting social setting, is self-regulation.

Social skill; this is the capacity to maintain interactions and manipulate individuals.

Empathy; it is the willingness to be considerate to the needs of other individuals, and to make choices that would benefit them.

Motivation; the motivating desire to accomplish those objectives.

Goleman and several other psychologists after he found that the emotionally intelligent person would absorb all the attributes. That means you can internalize self-awareness, self-regulation, cognitive skills, empathy and inspiration with concentrated effort.

CHAPTER 1

History of Emotional Intelligence

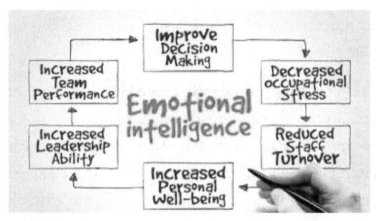

eter Salovey and John first invented the word
'emotional intelligence'

P
D. Mayer, in 1990, defined it as a sort of social
intelligence involving the ability to control one's own
emotions as well as the feelings and emotions of other
people, to distinguish between those emotions and to
use this knowledge to direct one's thoughts and
behavior.

Salovey and Mayer developed a study initiative to
assess and investigate the importance of a person's
emotional intelligence. For starters, a research was
performed on a community of individuals, where it was
found that people who can recognize and assign a

simple name to feelings might quickly rebound from a traumatic film they'd seen.

In another experiment, individuals who scored high in their ability to accurately interpret situations and recognize or recognize the feelings of other people were able to react more successfully to shifts within their social group and create social support networks.

During the early 90s, Daniel Goleman got acquainted with the study of Salovey and Mayer, which led him to the author Emotional Intelligence. Goleman's school of emotional intelligence concluded that it was not logical knowledge that assured the prosperity of a person's company, but the capacity of an individual to control the emotions of his own and of others that decided his chances of success. He said emotionally intelligent citizens possess four major features:

1. People with high emotional intelligence are excellent at recognizing their feelings, so they have clear knowledge of themselves.
2. They perfected the manageability of their feelings.
3. They have been trained to display concern with other people's feelings.

4. They were able to manage other's feelings successfully.

The seeds of emotional intelligence were sown long back in the 1930s when Edward Thorndike placed forth the idea of 'social intelligence.' He defined it as being capable of forming interpersonal and social relations with people.

David Wechsler proposed in the 1940s that effective intelligence qualities might be responsible for the success.

Humanist psychology Abraham Maslow also explained how individuals should develop mental intensity throughout the 1950s.

People began speaking about feelings and the mind in 1953. Dorothy Van Ghent has explained how characters of high emotional intelligence appeared in novels such as Jane Austen's Pride and Prejudice.

Howard Gardner published The Broken Mind in 1975 and explored the idea of various kinds of intelligence apart from cognitive intelligence.

Mensa Magazine released an essay in 1987, in which Keith Beasley first used "emotional quotient" as a term.

This was the first documented usage of the word, though in his unfinished research prior to the Mensa article Reuven Bar-on continued to use the phrase.

In 1990 the ground-breaking report on emotional intelligence by Peter Salovey and John Meyer was written.

In 1995, after the New York Times writer Daniel Goleman's publication of Emotional Intelligence: Why It Should Mean More Than IQ, the idea of Emotional Intelligence became worldwide popular. Goleman relied on Salovey and Meyer's studies to speak about emotional intelligence as a critical form of knowledge for academic and job achievement.

One of the most important features of emotional intelligence is that there is no set emotional intelligence unlike the intellect quotient. Although some born with an aptitude for different emotional and social aspects, emotional intelligence is mostly malleable.

Experts of emotional intelligence believe that traditional intelligence leads only 10-25 per cent to our performance. However, a large part of it is decided by many variables, like our capacity to control the feelings of our own and of other people.

Study conducted by Harvard alumni in multiple professions, including medicine and law, found that there was none, and at times a negative correlation between high entry test scores and achievement in different professions. This obviously indicates that a high quotient or awareness of intelligence alone does not decide the likelihood of an individual succeeding.

Study led by Dr. Travis Bradberry found that 90 per cent of an organization's top-performing employees exhibit high emotional intelligence.

People with a strong emotional quotient often receive $29,000 more a year than their low-emotional intelligence peers from the same field. Thus, not only are people with high emotional intelligence more effective and successful, but they also earn more money on average than people with low emotional intelligence.

CHAPTER 2

The Impact of Emotional Intelligence

Emotional intelligence differs considerably from normal intelligence. Also, it is calculated differently. The ranking is seen in most organizations as most companies know that people with high EQ do more on the job than people with high IQ do. This is because people who are emotionally savvy will stay calm under challenging circumstances. Even they can quickly settle disputes and direct others by example. Those staff are willing to make rational choices on behalf of the company, and to direct them along.

Hence EQ is a vital tool for administrators, corporate owners and professionals in human resources. Data reveals individuals with strong EQ perform well than those with poor EQ do. For this cause, emotional maturity is deemed a vital competency across all roles of leadership. It can be applied to different areas of organizations and life at large. Any of EQ's software contain the following.

Coaching- EQ is used to educate administrators about how to communicate with members of their staff. Coaching with emotional intelligence lets people develop stronger connections, strengthen teamwork and decision making, raise motivation and decrease stress levels.

Employment performance profiles – In the past, emotional intelligence was effectively used to build career profiles. These are utilized during recruiting by most organizations because they include interpersonal qualities which are important for each profile.

Production of skills – The bulk of high achieving executives are wiser than their peers. Emotional intelligence lets us work well by optimizing their ability.

Training-EQ may be used to improve expertise for workers and allow them and succeed on the job. This is done by professionals to provide customer input on a large variety of channels.

Team Bonding – Cognitive maturity has a significant influence on the participants of the team and how they interact. It improves work productivity and tends to develop effective communication skills. Any of Emotional Intelligence's beneficial impacts include:

- Lesson changed. Emotional intelligence is a clearly understood term

- Understanding. It is not inherited, and can be obtained quickly. When properly studied it will boost the personality of an individual

- Prevents harmful actions. Empathy is a trait of emotional intelligence. High emotional maturity, in most situations, turns into positive behavior.

- Improved connections within culture. People with high emotional intelligence will connect well with others.

Emotional Intelligence and Career Success

Until recently, employers believed that all of the technical skills required candidates to excel in job positions. The definition of emotional intelligence, though, has continually proven this is not valid. When it comes to market performance, human qualities are as essential as technological skills. Organizations today are searching for creative people that can connect well with peers and clients.

When you fully comprehend your feelings and learn how to control them, at the office, you'll easily get along with others. It is related by QE practitioners to improved work satisfaction and higher pay. While most people place great emphasis on IQ, its importance can never be effective without it being incorporated with EQ. One of EQ's leading scholars, Daniel Goleman, once hypothesized that emotional intelligence is as essential as IQ, in terms of job performance. In their professions, individuals who concentrate on improving their EQ on the job often grow faster than those who do not. If you're still thinking about being a great leader, you'll need to invest in developing your intellect.

In some people the ability to recognize your feelings, as well as those of others, can come naturally. Many businesses and organizations, using online assessment tools, are now focusing on developing this expertise for their workers. A vast array of professionals deliver these.

Emotional intelligence generally consists of four major competencies. Such are:

1. being self-conscious. As mentioned in chapter one, self-awareness relates to the capacity to consider our feelings and how they influence our response to the conditions and situations around us
2. Self-management. This is the capacity to regulate our feelings and to guide our characters positively and constructively
3. Social awareness, which means being able to connect with other people's emotions and be aware of their feelings and thoughts
4. Manage partnerships. This applies to the willingness to utilize the three aforementioned competencies to handle day-to-day experiences

Everyone has a diverse degree of emotional maturity. This can be improved though through different actions and preparation. There are some actions you should take as a professional individual and as a leader to ensure your emotional intelligence places you ahead of others

- Starting with knowing the emotions. If you have negative habits such as frustration and rage, for example, you should start learning ways to counteract this behavior

- Focus on knowing yourself and how the people around you perceive and behave. People struggle to express their feelings with their fellow workers in most workplace settings. Understanding other people's feelings and allowing them a chance to show themselves are some of the ways to create enduring partnerships.
- Put several relationship-building tactics, lastly. Know when to work alone, and when to work together with other people.

Following these actions is key to your future in the field. EQ has the capacity and influence to guide you into leadership positions within the enterprise. Most workers receiving good wages relate that to a high EQ. This is how they realize whether to apply for an increase of pay. They're not doing anything anyhow, so they're looking for the right time and the way they expect their bosses to do so. Easily, those workers often get wage raises and they are often more efficient than low-EQ staff. They even enjoy excellent credibility for their keen expertise in establishing partnerships.

Data currently reveals that just 15 percent of job achievement is due to professional abilities. The other

85% comes from intelligence, human relationships, and the ability to lead, connect, and compromise. That is how important the wisdom of the feeling is. Most successful leaders use their high EQ to create relationships that will help them uplift their professions. Strong EQ also places businesses on the cutting side. Many consumers buy a product from a salesperson, who will approach them on a personal level. This is why certain goods that aren't that successful sell higher than fantastic items.

Emotional Intelligence and Personal Relations

Human beings are beings which are sentimental. They can sometimes become antagonistic. You may meet any persons once in a while who do not respect you or those clients who regard you with disrespect. How you respond to those individuals will decide if your friendship with them is going to improve or deteriorate.

People always feel ignored and left out even if this is not the case. Such people suffer from the fear of speaking out in silence. Emotional intelligence helps you identify and inspire those individuals to become a better version of themselves. In today's world, resolving any emotional related issues is critical since people deal with tough situations on a daily basis. Helping people find a solution to their problems is desirable, because social awareness is one of the key components of emotional intelligence.

Each leader's aim is to cause impact. When put together, individual accomplishments translate into successful business or organization. Therefore maintaining good relationships with others is significant. You need to learn how to talk, connect and work with others to do that. Among the aspects that Daniel Goleman has highlighted that can help build your partnerships are:

- The self-confidence. That's the opportunity to consider and analyze before you act. Reliance on oneself is critical when coping with challenging circumstances or disputes
- Internal inspiration – that comes from inside a human. It applies to the desire to attain tasks for personal purposes, not that an incentive is linked to it
- Awareness-applies to the opportunity to recognize and inspire people around you. That's essential to leaders working with teams

- Social skills-capacity to shape partnerships and maintain them

Emotional Intelligence and the Workplace

EQ is considered by most analysts as one of the most important tools in the work world. This is because workers with high EQ ratings are best put under reduced to no monitoring to handle tension, work with their colleagues and complete tasks. They will benefit from their past failures, and create better preparations for the organization's future.

While high EQ is not necessary for every workplace, any job requiring contact with individuals needs emotionally smart workers. For example, real estate or sales agents expect strong communication and negotiating skills from individuals. These abilities don't usually require individualistic occupations such as analysis and accounting. It has also been observed that if highly intelligent workers are put in positions where they tend to work individually, they could be underperforming on the job since they may expend more time attempting to reach out to someone than completing their work.

EQ and Leadership Skills

Although emotional maturity can be optional for subordinate-level staff, it is of considerable value to those in leadership roles. To be effective, leaders must be able to communicate well with the citizens with whom they operate. Effective leaders also build a positive working atmosphere in which people feel respected, motivated and significant.

The best emotionally knowledgeable leaders have the potential to create trust in their staff. They see each person as an entity with special talents, attitudes and histories. They should not regard teams as a group and is standard. They often understand and relate the feelings of and member of the team by expressing both their fears and their joys.

It is especially necessary to be able to establish confidence with other workers when you have to expose them to a new idea. If the team likes you, it would be easy to encourage them to do something different, since they value your leadership.

Like any other partnership, partnerships in the workplace will undergo certain misunderstandings here and there. When it occurs, it can be fixed amicably by just emotionally informed officials, meaning that the people concerned are on good terms.

Good leaders are always brave in making their faults. By encouraging others to acquire certain EI skills from them, they can effectively improve work relationships this way. They will be able to train their brain by constant practice of what they are learning from you. They'll turn this into a routine quickly and you'll see a difference in their actions.

A chief who has low EQ still finds it hard to communicate to others. He's not going to be effective at recognizing the expectations and needs of those he commands. A leader who allows an emotional outburst without controlling it can create mistrust and disrespect among his subordinates. Such an activity will have a detrimental effect on other staff's mood, ethos, and meaning of the organization. Good leaders should consider how their interactions will affect the entire squad, whether verbal or non-verbal.

How does leadership appear like emotional intelligence? Emotional maturity may be detected in leadership by testing their attitudes, according to Daniel Goleman. Among the typical attributes are:

- From front end. Being the Team an example. Inspire them to work on the collective purpose
- Confidence, integrity and honesty; both are characteristics of self-confidence
- Outstanding listening skills. Emotionally wise leaders are quick to reach and are optimistic
- Choices are straight forward, straightforward and logical
- Empathy and Effects

Clearly, technological expertise and abilities cannot deliver such qualities and anything else. Nutshell, emotionally wise representatives are showing this by their acts and speech.

Emotional Intelligence and Mental Health

The understanding of mental health is one of the facets of EQ which has been growing. In humans of all ages, races, occupations and gender identities, mental instability is normal. There are several issues that cause this, and no single case can be treated the same way as the other.

In some of the strategies employed, emotional intelligence was effectively used to support people with mental health problems. While EQ cannot take the place of medical treatment and therapy, some of the signs of such problems can be avoided.

One of the things engaged in this field is self-awareness. Self-consciousness helps one to examine one's own feelings and their impact on overall well-being. Mental health professionals are utilizing this factor to help people understand their existing situation. Being a core component of EQ, self-awareness enables people who are at the lowest mental health thresholds to become aware of their emotions. It also allows them to get their dilemma acknowledged and dealt with in good time. EQ was also effectively utilized as a preventive measure against mental illness.

Therefore it is important to implement self-awareness when it comes to psychological and emotional equilibrium. Beneficiaries should prevent stress-inducing tasks and activities. They also learn how to focus on places in which they do better, and use them to build confidence. They are able to enhance their attitude by building their confidence, and remain happy most of the time.

Good mental health centers round being able to manage one's emotions. Based on the experiences and obstacles you come through, the feelings will keep changing throughout the day.

Mental problems can be considered to be minor issues but when you are unable to deal with them, they become a worry. Controlling one's feelings isn't an easy task, but for it to become a routine it should be exercised constantly. Some of the techniques used for this include deep relaxation, concentration, reflection, self-talking and setting objectives.

- Target building – this encourages you to recover focus and lets you work on achieving the activities. Attaining these targets will help you recover control over your emotions
- Mindfulness-allows you to enjoy the moment. It discourages you from reflecting on previous mistakes, or thinking on the future. Mindfulness lets you reflect on meeting your current objectives. It gives you the courage to cope with current circumstances.
- Intense respiration – helps you to recover in tense periods. It offers you more power of your body and your mind. Even sleep does the same. It lets you relax and collect the resources needed to execute those tasks

- Positive self-talk – prevents you from building up unpleasant experiences and circumstances feelings. An individual with mental health problems may find it hard to change his or her way of thinking. Small, subtle improvements will make a major difference however.

You will learn to become emotionally aware when confronted with a mental struggle by integrating some of your core feelings, recognizing that they are part of you, and determining how they affect your behavior and decisions.

Teamwork and relational maturity

Research years now prove emotional intelligence is a critical component of team success. It is influencing how team members handle their attitudes and vulnerabilities. It also affects their choices, which helps them achieve positive outcomes. Highly smart teams will often build an exciting work atmosphere which contributes to improved productivity.

Individuals who know how to control their own feelings and other people's emotions still make great members of the team. Just like emotionally smart bosses, extremely smart teams can perform difficult challenges, solve conflicts and motivate each other to accomplish team goals. Some of the widely utilized main EI skills in teams include communication skills, empathy and emotional control. Unfortunately certain qualities are always absent in some of the team members, making teamwork impossible. This is because participants of low Fit teams also trigger in-team confusion, disagreements and uncertainty.

Emotional intelligence promotes organizational objective coordination. You've definitely come across a workplace along your career path, where morale is low, and there's tension among group members. In some organizations this is normal and the best way to overcome it is by creating a positive work environment that encourages employees. This can be accomplished through some common methods, such as activities in team-building. This not only improves team morale but equips them with the requisite emotional intelligence skills as well.

Emotional intelligence helps teams improve their overall approach and attitude towards community and each other's tasks. It helps to regulate the feelings at the team level, resulting in more respect and confidence. Building trust within a team can be a slow process, but if you want to achieve progress, it is important that you do this. A team can have everything it needs to succeed but is still struggling because of the lack of emotional intelligence.

Lack of communication generally for team members is one of the pillars of issues. Misunderstandings and low workplace communication lead to bitterness, anger and team confusion. Effective communication helps you crack down walls. It also allows teams to develop stronger relationships when both within the organization and within departments, workers can better understand their task. As staff understand their role and overall value within the organization, they can find it easy to accept the corporate vision and direction. Getting such a shared sense of purpose is what helps in stabilizing the market and enhancing team performance.

In effective communication emotional intelligence plays a major role. It helps teams to build more productive workplaces and a better culture of organization.

Emotional Intelligence and Life Achievements

There are people from a young age who exhibit emotional intelligence. Such people are always acknowledged and are patient with peers. Also they tend to be calmer when under pressure. All of these can be signs of high EQ, and can lead to great achievements in life if properly steered.

In the society emotional intelligence has been a stepchild for a long time. Most parents were unable to associate that concept with their highly smart children. This is because the EQ was not valued; nor had it been developed in early career and childhood training. For this reason IQ has been the only tool used to measure success for quite some time.

Also emotions can be portrayed as organized responses. They're common in systems of motivation, cognition, and physiology. They are always stirred in response to occurrences or events, which may be either internal or external. How an individual brings forth his emotions determines whether they will influence others positively or negatively.

Measuring Emotional Intelligence

The measurement of emotional intelligence varies depending on the components and abilities that you wish to test. Given that intelligence is involved in this concept, EI can only be evaluated for accuracy by evaluating the responses given by respondents. Some of the traditional instruments used for assessing emotional intelligence include:

1. Baron EQi-This is a self-completed exam that assists in evaluating such competencies such as empathy, problem solving, sensitivity and satisfaction. Emotional intelligence, according to this evaluation, consists of many cognitive and non-cognitive capacities and skills that affect the capacity to manage demands and stresses.

2. SASQ-SASQ is a questionnaire in Selgman attribution type. It consisted of a screening procedure which is used to assess degrees of hope and pessimism in individuals and communities.

3. MEIS – This is the emotional intelligence measure multifactor that incorporates measures

used to determine the capacity of an individual to recognize, recognize and control emotions.

4. Emotional Competency Inventory or ECI also utilizes a test for self-assessment to score strengths across a variety of emotional competencies.

Multiple tests are used to assess various facets of the mental intellect and attitude.

Test outcomes

EQ test results are, in most situations, the expertise needed to decide whether a person is emotionally intelligent or not. These abilities include emotional self-consciousness, emotional communication, other-consciousness, moral logic and self-management. Emotional expression relates to the capacity to communicate or convey yourself efficiently. That characteristic is what helps people and teams understand each other. It creates trust and genuineness in teams, too. Emotional judgment is the capacity to make choices using emotional intelligence.

High emotional rationale leads to better decision making.

Emotional self-regulation often exists and relates to the ability to regulate one's emotions. Self-control increases your physical well-being when practiced properly, which helps you to think objectively even under difficult situations. It also makes you feel positive in coping with circumstances.

These are some of the things you can use to classify the emotional quotient.

- Self-reflection. People use this tool to represent their daily behavior, and to score their results. These practices lead to concerns such as 'how do you see yourself,' 'what do people think of you,' and 'what do you gain by analyzing your behavior.'
- The test of personality. These are designed to identify behavioral patterns which determine your type of personality
- Power testing. This are used for assessing strengths and weaknesses in persons. They further explain how these can be matched to effectiveness.
- Individual values. This is where you identify and evaluate your personal values, in terms of how important they are to you. It's also possible

to combine ideals and personal visions and establish an ideal future for oneself and how it can be done.

- Journaling. This means bringing together the ideas and emotions in a journal, diary or newspaper and eventually quantifying them into acts and outcomes. You will do this to set up your own unique story. You will also use this to determine whether there are any behavioral dynamics and behaviors in which to enhance results.

These exercises assess your EQ, and help you to better grasp your personality. You will use these to boost your EQ and create more awareness about yourself.

How to Put Emotional Intelligence in Practice

It is one thing to be emotionally intelligent when having EQ components at work is another. For e.g., tension is known to confuse a lot of people's thinking. By improving your emotional intelligence you will quickly reduce your stress levels. Life contains numerous difficult moments which may cause moments of stress. When you are nervous, being have in the right way becomes complicated for you. Using emotional intelligence to alleviate tension involves identifying anything that causes the stress and figuring out ways to resolve it. You should come up with a list of hobbies and stuff that can help relieve tension, including going out with friends or taking a walk. If this is not effective then you may be forced to seek professional assistance. You can be advised by a counselor or behavioral consultant about how to boost the moral quotient as a way to deal with stress.

Emotional maturity parallels light-heartedness. Light-hearted people are always hopeful, and find it easy to feel life's positivity. People that are hopeful prefer to experience better mental well-being than people that are often cynical towards all. This is because cynical individuals are just forecasting errors and dwelling on what goes bad instead of appreciating what goes right. People are still content with happiness. They use humor to solve stressful times and still help people feel comfortable.

What Emotionally Intelligent People Avoid

Emotions will also have a toll on you and you can lose balance and behave emotionally if you don't hold them in place. Despite this, individuals who are socially savvy are also conscious of how they make others feel. They seem to care more about how they affect them than they do about how others impact them. There are some features which they usually prevent. Let's have a peek at those.

• Evite drama

While individuals with high EQ listen to others and extend empathy to them, they do not enable the desires, opinions, and emotions of others to overrule their own desires.

• They rarely complain

Extremely smart people are recognized for their optimistic outlook. They may be oppressed and may find a response to their problems but the sense of failure and victimization is unusual for them to convey. It's not usual for them to throw in the towel and to announce publicly that a challenge is beyond their capacity. This makes it impossible for them to accuse others for their failures and misfortunes as they are doing it with their struggles and finding private remedies.

• Not allowing emotions to dominate them

While emotionally intelligent people understand the power of working out their emotions, it is not normal for them to cause their decisions and judgments to be guided by these sentiments. Emotions are vital in day-to-day activities and interactions; however, they can drive you into damaging conduct and relationships if left untamed. This is why extremely smart people don't want feelings to control their way of life.

They can easily overcome because they've spent time knowing their feelings and how this behavior is having an impact. They place sense above emotions and are therefore able to align themselves and surmount the underlying circumstances.

• Stops criticism

People with emotional smartness will quickly suppress suicidal feelings. They may acknowledge the possibility that negative thoughts will emerge but do not weigh this in their way of living and making decisions. They still take responsibility, without criticizing others, for their feelings and actions. This is because they truly realize that they have the ability to decide how they react to significant shifts in their lives and surroundings.

People with high EQ realize that playing the victim and accusing someone just destroys partnerships it doesn't fix the issue.

• They do not live on the past

A decent amount of extremely smart individuals are just gaining about their failures but are not focusing on them. They realize that their decisions are the product of the outcome, and that little can be done to alter the outcome. Yet they're utilizing previous perspectives to form the future.

• Doesn't cover emotions

They are not avoiding how they felt. Unlike people with low EQ who can face difficulties in silence, people who are extremely smart stop masking their sensations. They realize how their emotions can be distorted and can affect their overall health. They recognize the feelings ought to be allowed out and conveyed in a fashion that relieves them and assures that they stay emotionally, physically and psychologically healthy.

• Evicting selfishness

People with emotional intelligence tend to be greedy. They recognize empathy's role in relationships, and they realize the harmful consequences of selfishness. Therefore, they recognize other people's needs and strive for satisfying those needs

• Evicting social pressure

They should not cause the views and creeds of other cultures to influence their judgment. They don't depend on the views of others to make important choices when confronted with an obstacle. Many individuals who are emotionally wise function differently and don't obey the herd. They don't do anything solely because other people do so.

• Stops being too negative

They should not blame others who have suffered, and they recognize the value of each individual of a team. Criticism destroys morality in an individual. Since they respect partnerships and support each other, they still insist on getting the most out of the mistakes of others. They realize that people are not equal, and can make errors without really realizing them.

• They never offer reasons for their emotions

Emotionally smart people place considerable importance on their feelings. We are also mindful of the reality that the human race will continue to have feelings. They experience sorrow, rage, hurt and discomfort almost as well as they can keep in control. They understand that this is a normal phenomenon, and are trying to resolve the emotional side of those emotions. They accept the actual circumstance and freely share certain feelings as the need emerges. They recognize that life is full of difficulties in general and that feelings are valuable to express how they feel about these obstacles.

• They are not searching for pleasure but are building pleasure

Person satisfaction with low EQ is also linked to people, situations and incidents. For emotionally aware persons the reverse is real. They depend on nothing for their happiness. They seldom ask other people about help, and they realize the inspiration comes from inside. They still aspire to build a healthy atmosphere, overflowing with fun and laughter. Their contentment comes from inside. People who are emotionally wise never let someone spoil their day. They are always able to remain focused on the main objective of being positive and though things get difficult. They know satisfaction is something nobody else can give. Therefore they perpetuate it on their own and by definition affect others.

As a person trying to learn more about emotional intelligence, whether you want to achieve your maximum ability, you should often prevent those habits.

How to Boost Your Emotional Intelligence

To improve your emotional intelligence all you need is a desire to do so. Start paying attention to how people conduct themselves, how you act and react and try to put yourself in the shoes of others. Training to empathize is perhaps the best way to start improving your own emotional intelligence, and how you do company makes a huge difference.

Take some time to evaluate your business relationships according to the many advantages I've listed in this post. Map your own advances. You could even spend a week on every factor that you wish to improve. You can do that, and since the advantages of emotional intelligence are so important to the business success I'd get started right away!

To increase the degree of Emotional Intelligence, you must become self-conscious about the feelings you are feeling at any given time, and you must also cope with the emotions you have hidden in an attempt to escape confronting them. It's a common tendency to want to drive a certain emotion down or to reassure yourself that you're not feeling a particular emotion because it's painful or that emotion feels unacceptable under the conditions for some occasion. Emotional Intelligence allows you to be aware of your own emotions and know how to manage them.

That is not something you can do automatically-it's an operation. To conclude this step effectively it would help to recall the following emotional facts:

Emotional intelligence is based on adaptation

Emotional Intelligence varies from normal or traditional intelligence in that you can basically increase your Emotional Intelligence at will. And becoming emotionally wise is an important aspect of establishing good connections with families, acquaintances and colleagues. Individuals with high emotional intelligence are praised for being consistent, cool, composed, and safe, and also possessing an intuitive ability to understand others. We still appear to know what to do in any particular circumstance, since they are not distracted with their feelings, and they can think more objectively and behave more appropriately.

Emotions change constantly

Making your emotions self-aware, and what triggers them, is not the same as dwelling on them. Take note of how the different things that you do on every particular day trigger one emotion to emerge and another to subside and you will see that feelings are always subject to change.

Sometimes, the feelings are linked to physical sensation

You have probably noticed that the way the body reacts to the emotion of fear is different from the emotion of pleasure, that when you're relaxed, the way you feel emotionally is different from when you're upset, etc. For example, paying attention to the fact that your hands are shaking, that your muscles are tense, and that your heart beats quickly, all of which are tied to fear, will help you realize why you're afraid and help you manage that fear so that you can deal with it constructively.

Emotional intelligence is no match for justification & reasoning

It will become practically natural to become conscious of what emotions and feelings you are having, and to know how to manage certain emotions and feelings. Once you no longer struggle to deal naturally with your emotions and feelings, the ability to think and reason is easier and more reliable and you can use it to move with your emotions without being overwhelmed by them. You will become stronger at this just like anything else when you practice, practice and keep practicing.

When we have an awareness of your feelings, what they are, and how they influence us, we build the foundation to be aware of ourselves. Self-management then follows with a differing set of competencies taking us further down the path of raising your emotional intelligence.

CHAPTER 3

Attributes of Emotional Intelligence

Empathy

Emotional intelligence has the following attributes

- Self-awareness
- Empathy
- Motivation
- Self-regulation
- Social skills

Self-awareness

Simply put, self-awareness is consciousness of oneself, with the self-being that makes one's personality unique. These unique elements include ideas, experiences and competencies. More emotional intelligence makes him more self-conscious within an individual.

The research of the subjective self-awareness can be tracked back to 1972. Psychologists Shelley Duval and Robert Wick Lund developed the Theory of Auto-Consciousness.

They proposed: "As we reflect on ourselves, we evaluate and compare our current behavior with our own standards and values. We are self-conscious as impartial evaluators of ourselves." Essentially, they see self-consciousness as a significant component of self-control.

Daniel Goleman proposed a definition of self-awareness as "knowing one's internal conditions, decisions, abilities and intuitions," which places greater emphasis on the ability to track our inner world, our thoughts and emotions when they occur.

Knowing that self-awareness is not just about what we think about ourselves but also about how we perceive and track our inner world.

Have you ever made a decision about your own thoughts or experiences? If indeed, then you are not alone and now is the time to work towards a non-judgmental self-reflection.

Of course this is said more quickly than achieved.

Since non-judgmental honesty is a critical component of self-awareness, how do we move towards it? When we realize what is occurring inside of us, we will understand them and embrace them as the inevitable part of being human, rather than give ourselves a difficult time.

If you ever said to yourself, "I should / shouldn't have done it," so you know what that means. The next time you assess something you've said or done, consider the question: "Is what I've learned an opportunity to learn and grow, too? Have other people made a similar mistake and benefited from it?" Self-awareness goes beyond gaining self-knowledge: it's also about paying attention to our inner state, with a beginner's mind and an open heart.

Our mind is highly skilled at preserving knowledge on how we react to a given incident to create a model for our emotional existence. This awareness often ends up influencing our minds in order to react in a way like in the future; we are witnessing a similar occurrence.

Self-consciousness allows one to be mindful of this unconscious repression and preconceptions and may form the foundation for freeing the mind from it.

Will Self-awareness Matter?

Self-awareness is the core component of the mental intelligence, according to Daniel Goleman.

The willingness to monitor our feelings and perceptions from moment to moment is necessary to truly understand ourselves, to be at ease with who we are, and to proactively regulate our thoughts, emotions and behaviors.

In comparison, individuals who are self-conscious prefer to behave actively (instead of unconsciously reacting) and appear to be in good health, and have a healthy perception of life. You also have a richer life experience and are more likely to feel more forgiving.

Sutton's inquiry (2016) has explored the constituent parts of self-awareness and its effects.

This study found that aspects of self-consciousness, self-reflection, intuition, and perception can lead to benefits such as becoming a more compassionate individual, whereas aspects of rumination and comprehension may lead to psychological burdens.

Various study has identified self-awareness as a key characteristic of effective entrepreneurs. A research by Green Peak Collaborators and Cornell University researched 72 executives in both public and private corporations. They had all profited from $50 million to $ 5 billion, and it was discovered that "the strongest predictor of overall success was a large self-awareness ranking. In this study, self-awareness — was the greatest predictor of overall success.

Self-consciousness is often important for psychotherapists.

"Therapists need to recognize their own perceptions, ideals, traditional beliefs and assumptions in order to appropriately support culturally diverse clients" (Oden et al., 2009).

It has also been considered a "precursor to multicultural skills" (Buckley & Foldy, 2010). In other terms, self-awareness allows clinicians to understand the differences in their perspectives and the situations their clients have been through.

Which will help psychologists keep their customers less judgmental and allow them truly appreciate their customers.

Why is Self-conscious Hard?

If self-awareness is so essential, then why are we not more self-aware?

The most obvious answer is that we're really "not there" for studying ourselves most of the time. In other words, we're not there to pay attention to what's happening inside or around us.

Psychologists Matthew Kills worth and Daniel T. Gilbert find that about half of the time, we 're working on "automatic pilot" or unaware about what we're doing or how we behave, while our mind wanders about something other but here and now.

Besides the frequent roaming of mind, our capacity to provide a clear view of ourselves is also influenced by the various cognitive bias; we prefer to accept narratives which reinforce our already established sense of self.

For example, if we are strongly convinced that we are a high-quality and loyal friend, then we are likely to interpret events — even events where we may have made a mistake — as an affirmation in our reputation as that "honest friend." This pre-existing confidence in ourselves will influence how we treat the consequences of, say, losing a lunch date with a buddy.

Furthermore, confirmation bias can trick us into looking for or viewing information in a way that reinforces our preconception of something. Have you ever had the feeling when you approved a job offer but are still checking for extra evidence that this is the perfect job for you?

Moreover, the lack of willingness to receive input could also be acting against us if we want a more detailed view of ourselves through the eyes of others.

When we try to develop our own self-awareness, how can we balance it with certain unconscious patterns it accept only those representations of ourselves?

It's not easy but there are some options. What further complicates the picture is the different aspects of the self that we contribute to in everyday life.

Daniel Kahneman is Nobel Prize laureate for his contribution to cognitive science.

Kahneman addresses the difference between the "experiencing self" and the "remembering self" and how it affects our decision-making. He describes how we feel regarding the encounter at the moment and how we remember the event may be somewhat different and share about 50 percent of the connection.

This distinction can have a huge impact on the story we tell ourselves, the way we connect to ourselves and others, and the choice we make, even though we may not notice the difference most of the time.

Cultivating Self-Awareness

Ways to create some space for yourself. It's hard to see things clearly when you're in a dark room without windows. The space you create is that gap on the wall where you allow light to pass through. Stay away from digital distractions and spend some time with yourself, reading, writing, meditating and communicating with yourself — maybe first thing in the morning or half an hour before sleeping.

Practice mindfulness

Mindfulness is the essence to self-confidence. Jon Kabat-Zinn describes mindfulness as "to pay attention in a particular way, consciously, in the present moment, without judging." By cultivating awareness, you'll be more in yourself, so that you can "be there" and know what's going on in and around you. It's not about sitting with your legs crossed or ignoring your emotions.

Keep a log

Writing not just lets us express our feelings but also allows us closer to ourselves and at peace. Writing can create more headspace as well as having the emotions flow on paper. Evidence suggests that writing about stuff we're thankful for or also problems we're dealing with lets improve satisfaction and contentment.

Train as a strong listener

Listening is not quite the same as listening. Listening is about being present, paying full attention to other people's emotions, body movement, and language. It is about showing empathy and understanding without constantly evaluating or judging. You'll also be better at listening to your own inner voice when you become a good listener and your own best friend.

Request Reviews

Sometimes we can be too afraid to question what people think about us—yes, often the responses might be skewed or even misleading, but once you understand more about yourself and others, you'll be able to distinguish them from actual and sincere input. Research has shown that getting 360-degree reviews in the workplace is a valuable method for enhancing managers' self-awareness (Jessi) (Source)

Empathy

Empathy is used to describe a wide array of experiences. Emotional researchers typically describe empathy as the ability to perceive other people's feelings, combined with the ability to anticipate what others may think or feel.

Contemporary scholars also differentiate between two forms of empathy: "Affective empathy" applies to the impressions and feelings we get while listening to others' emotions; this may involve mirroring what the person feels or actually getting overwhelmed while sensing another's discomfort or anxiety. Cognitive empathy, also called "perspective take," implies our capacity to explore and appreciate other people's feelings. Studies show a tough time empathizing with those with autism spectrum conditions.

Empathy has significant origins in our minds and bodies, both in our evolutionary past. Elementary types of empathy have been found in our primate relatives, in dogs and even in rodents. Empathy has been associated with two different brain circuits and scientists have proposed that some aspects of empathy can be linked to mirror cells of mind that fire when we see someone else performing an action in much the same manner they will fire if we undertook the action ourselves. Analysis has also uncovered signs of a genetic foundation for empathy, while studies indicate that individuals can boost (or limit) their natural empathy.

Getting empathy does not always imply we would choose to support those in distress, but it is always a crucial first move in compassionate action. Empathy is a building stone of morality — for individuals who obey the Universal Law, it helps because they can place themselves in someone else's shoes. It is also a vital component of good partnerships, as it makes one consider the views, desires and goals of other individuals. Here are a few examples the science has shown empathy's far-reaching value.

Empathy may be infectious

As group standards promote empathy, it is more likely that people will be empathic — and more altruistic.

Empathy reduces bigotry and racism in a study, white participants forced to empathize with an African American man subsequently showed fewer racial bias from these early types of empathy, research indicates that we will establish more nuanced mechanisms which go a long way towards improving our ties and the environment around us. Indeed, study shows learning empathy lets one consider the experiences of other individuals by not getting stressed as we experience their negative feelings.

Get ahead of yourself:

Research demonstrates that we will raise our own degree of empathy by consciously considering what someone may be feeling.

Don't leap on other conclusions:

We have no understanding because we presume those who are hurting receive what they earn in every way.

Show empathetic body language

Empathy is communicated not only by what we hear, but also through our facial gestures, pose, tone of voice and (or lack of) contact with the ears.

Take meditation

Richard Davidson's neuroscience research indicates that meditation — specifically loving-kindness meditation based on caring for others — could increase the capacity for empathy in both short-term and long-term meditators (although particularly in long-term meditators).

Discover imaginary worlds: Keith Oatley and their collaborators have discovered that people who read novels are more attuned to other people's feelings and behavior.

Play games

Neuroscience research suggests that when we interact against others our minds create a "mental model" of the other person's thoughts and actions.

Take lessons for infant

Mary Gordon's Roots of Empathy initiative aims to boost empathy by introducing infants into schools, encouraging the children's basic ability to identify with other people's emotions.

Research has shown that reaching a higher socioeconomic status lowers empathy, perhaps because people with high SES feel less need to communicate, depend on or collaborate with others. As the divide between the haves and the have-nots is widening, we risk seeing an empathy deficit as well. This doesn't mean money is evil, but if you've got a lot of it, you may need to be more willing to keep your own conscience for others.

Be wary about expressions

Paul Ekman's groundbreaking analysis has shown we can enhance our capacity to recognize other people's feelings by regularly observing facial expressions.

One should learn to accept empathy

People who believe their empathy level is growing put more time into becoming empathetic, listening to others and caring even though it's challenging (What is empathy?).

Motivation

People with high EI are willing to defer immediate results for long-term success. They are highly productive, they love a challenge, and they are competitive at anything they do.

Motivation is an internal process. If we describe it as a motive or a need, motivation is a state within us that requires an improvement, be it in the self or the world. Motivation pushes the individual with the drive and motivation required to engage with the world in a flexible, open-ended, and problem-solving manner as we tap into this energy well (Reeve, 2018).

The nature of inspiration is energized, and consistent goal-directed behavior. When we're inspired, we behave and step on.

Motivation is driven by the fulfillment of needs which are either necessary for sustaining life or significant for wellbeing and development. Physiological needs for food, water, and shelter help the organism to preserve life and also provide pleasure.

Psychological self-reliance, superiority and belonging desires drive our actions in much the same way. Strength, resolution, sense, and self-esteem, just like accomplishment requires to. Some of these needs will become motives, as with all the intrinsic activities that we engage in.

Our environment and social background can play a significant role as regards extrinsic motivation. We will also be inspired to feel specific emotions related to certain goals, values and wishes of the end-state (Reeve, 2018).

In everyday life, inspiration is best explained when you see what it looks like. Here is an explanation of a person's motivating motives to indulge in exercise. The analysis of motivation in psychology is about giving the best potential responses to two big questions:

What induces the unusual actions, and why does the severity of behavior vary?

Motivational psychology is a behavioral science that seeks to develop theories on what induces human motivation, and how motivational processes operate.

Viewed in the real world and evaluated through research, motivation is evident and measurable through behavior, level of commitment, neural stimulation, and psychophysiology. Others may include self-reporting in this category as well, but studies have found that self-reporting knowledge outlets have proven particularly inaccurate (Reeve, 2018). And how is inspiration doing itself? Of appearance, strength and consistency. Motivation is conveyed through movements and facial expressions, commitment, immediacy (or the psychologists prefer to term fast latency).

The motive in selecting one target over another can be derived from the rate of commitment and decision-making, which together allow for a strong likelihood of incidence.

Even the degree of dedication will indicate encouragement.

For e.g., a trained practitioner may consciously and enthusiastically add to the flow of conversation (argentic engagement), show curiosity and enjoyment (emotional engagement), consider deeply and pay attention (cognitive engagement) in a coaching scenario or motivational interview, and continue in such activities as if there were no time and outer environment (behavioral engagement)

Motivation Model

In summary, motivations are inward interactions in the context of desires, intellect, and feelings, and they are the driven action's immediate and proximal causes. Internal and social factors function as antecedents of motivations that induce or activate emotional processes. Our motivations are conveyed by actions, dedication, psychophysiology, stimulation of the brain and self-report.

Motivational counselors research the mechanism of motivation and its elements and aim to find the solution to the questions of what induces motivation. It also reveals that motivation research is so important to the lives of people and how inspiration positively contributes to meaningful life results such as achievement, productivity and well-being.

Motivation Process

Our motivation is always viewed as more urgent and strong because it derives from internal motives which are classified into desires, cognitions and emotions

Because we do not exist in a bubble, moreover, these inner experiences cannot take place without any degree of external control, whether in the form of consequences, incentives, or other forms of stresses arising from the social background of our setting.

Our physiological and psychological conditions motivate us, our cognitions direct us, and the feelings of land power and energy control our behaviors. As the mixture of antecedent circumstances and internal motivations match, they establish a fertile atmosphere of interaction that propels the action's actions.

Moreover, as those activities generate more desirable cognitive and emotional effects, they promote acts into a constructive reinforcement system and raise the probability of relapse (Reeve, 2018).

Find a question of encouragement such as procrastination, or evasion.

In procrastination or denial our desires, cognitions, feelings, environments, and relationships may play a crucial role.

All needs are born either from vulnerabilities or from which need. Physiological criteria are a highly effective element in assessing behavior. For example, our bodies can warn our brain if our well-being is compromised, and if we suffer from hunger, fatigue or lack of sleep this will contribute to evasion and procrastination.

Psychological concerns are often essential motivation generators, since they reflect an inborn desire to establish a sense of control, competency and communication. It can be difficult to resolve those irrational forces as we want to push ourselves to do something that satisfies such needs.

The tension between the desired action and the need to fulfill psychological needs, such as control, may cause dissonance, which can contribute to evasion or procrastination. If it is about maintaining health to satisfy physiological wishes, it is about thriving and evolving as a person to meet psychological needs

If we can no longer change a specific circumstance in life, we are forced to improve ourselves. Also there are tacit requirements learned from our community through socio-emotional development. As our perceptions differ, they vary from individual to individual, and tacit motivations are gained in relation to inborn psychological needs. Implicit here means mischievous. These desires are not actively mindful of, and they are trait-like and lasting. Implicit circumstances encourage us to explore specific social resources and to pursue them (Schultheiss & Brunstein, 2010).

An implicit motivation is a psychological imperative arising from emotional reaction-causing behavioral signals that then anticipate, direct and justify people's actions and lifestyle. They can be deduced from the person's signature feelings, attitudes, and behaviors. What an individual "gets" to undergo an affective or emotional trend is a tacit motivation.

For example, if we have little desire for success, we can feel detrimental consequences such as guilt, fear, and humiliation when we participate in this demanding mission, and therefore postpone to postpone it. Implicit motivations forecast our actions much more reliably than overt reasons, which are in effect what we inform ourselves of what motivates us.

And our cognitions can trigger our habit towards ignoring or procrastinating. Cognitions are conceptual structures such as objectives, attitude, perceptions, values and self-concept, to list only a few that impact our motivation. For e.g., we will be more inclined to delay or procrastinate if we have competing expectations.

Emotions

Emotions may be encouraging or demotivating because they are directly related to awareness and psychological needs. They may indicate the significance of a specific behavior. By engaging in a particular action we either feel joy or satisfaction in achieving the goal, or we may be afraid of failure and choose to stop or shy away.

Our environments

Our world can also be an optimal and supportive environment or a deterrent to staying motivated and attaining our objectives. It may be full of obstacles or situations allowing for continuous inspiration.

Relationships

Finally our partnerships should be positive and encouraging when it comes to transition. This can be clarified by a definition like a Michelangelo effect, where our connections support our ability. They may also be demotivating as in the Blueberry case, where the friendship is the worst in us and can result in procrastination and avoidance.

The Circle of Motivation

Motivation is a dynamic process, and our motivations are variable over time. Rise and fall as circumstances change, and motives are linked to the ongoing behavioral pattern as time passes. To make matters more difficult we are driven by a multitude of different motives at any given point in time.

One motivation will be highest and consume our focus, typically the most situational appropriate one, while other motivations will be comparatively latent and subordinate. While the highest motivation would usually have the most significant influence on our behavior when circumstances change, each subordinate motive may become dominant. Sensitivity about how inspiration changes over time is particularly important when setting goals.

When differentiating the motivating and performance-based gains and negatives among anyone that support a short-term target, such as consuming fewer than 2000 calories today against athletes that adopt a long-term aim, such as this year's reduction of 20 pounds, we ought to recognize the level of exercise they indulge in before providing suggestions.

Short-term targets perform well with uninteresting tasks as they improve motivation by offering input on success more regularly, thus enhancing attempts to continue (Reeve, 2018).

Motivation to conduct repetitive or tedious tasks may be improved, though, by offering clarification of expectations and decisions on how to accomplish a mission. Clarity and option may feel a sense of dominance and power, and as they satisfy basic psychological needs, both can increase overall motivation in turn.

Long-term goals work better when it comes to interesting initiatives, or as Mihaly Csikszentmihalyi (1990) calls them autotelic stuff, because they often have more stability and more discretion as to how to achieve them. Short term achievements may sound distracting for fascinating events. Autotelic practices are stimulating, and when they offer joy we are also profoundly inspired to carry them out. Perhaps most critically, we are driven to seek them, despite the lack of potential benefits or advantages. We must bear in mind that motivation to act on the goals is often more so when the goal is based in the future, while far-reaching goals do not build the tension of urgency that would motivate us to act immediately (Beata Souders, 2019)

Self-regulation

What Is Self-regulation? Andrea Bell has a clear self-regulation definition: It's self-control (2016).

As Bell also points out: "Whoever has good emotional self-regulation has the ability to keep their emotions in check. They can avoid impulsive behaviors that might make their condition worse, and when they feel down they can cheer up. They have a diverse repertoire of emotional and behavioral reactions that are well tailored to the demands of their environment"(2016).

Many types of therapy aim to enhance an individual's ability to self-regulate and restore a sense of control over one's actions and existence. Psychologists may use the word "self-regulation" to refer to one of two things:

Self-regulation of the behavior or self-regulation of the feelings.

We can dig at the disparity between the two below.

What is Behavioral Self-regulation?

It's the desire to behave with your best interests for the long run, with line with your core beliefs "(Stosny, 2011). That's what helps us sound in one way but behave in another.

If you've ever hated waking up and heading to work in the morning but persuaded yourself to do so by recalling your objectives (e.g. growing, promotion) or fundamental requirements (e.g. food, shelter), you've demonstrated good behavioral self-regulation.

What Is Self-Regulation in Emotion?

Emotional self-regulation, on the other hand, includes regulating the emotions – or at least manipulating them.

You have demonstrated good self-regulation of the feelings whether you have ever talked out of a negative mood or cooled down while you are upset.

What is the Self-Regulation Theory?

The self-regulation theory (SRT) specifically defines the process and components involved in choosing whether to think, do, speak, and do. It is especially notable when it comes to making a healthier decision because, for example, we have a deep urge to do the contrary, not to consume a whole pizza simply because it sounds nice.

According to modern SRT specialist Roy Baumeister (2007) 4 components are involved:

Desirable standards of conduct, incentive to meet standards,

Monitoring conditions and emotions before breaking expectations, vigilance that demands regulation of one's inner strength.

These four components combine at any given time to determine our self-regulatory conduct. In SRT terms, our behavior is determined by the personal levels of good behavior, our willingness to reach certain thresholds, the degree to which we are consciously aware of our situations and behaviors and the extent to which we are able to overcome the temptations and choose the best course.

The psychology of self-regulation

Self-regulation is an evolving phase in which we: According to Albert Bandura, a self-efficacy specialist and leading SRT researcher.

Track our actions, the behavioral factors and the behavioral results;

Assess our actions against our own personal standards and higher, more realistic norms;

Respond to our own behaviors;

Bandura further notes that self-efficacy plays a major role and influences our emotions, feelings, motivations and behavior.

The definition of self-efficacy can be explained by a simple thought experiment: Imagine two people who are highly driven to lose weight. They each track their food intake and exercise habits and have specific, measurable goals they set for themselves.

One of them has a large degree of self-efficacy and believes that if he puts an initiative into doing so, he will lose weight. The other has low self-efficacy and thinks like he can't keep to his recommended weight loss plan.

Who do you think will better say no to desserts? Which one you believe will be more successful in getting up to exercise early each morning?

We may tell with reasonable certainty that the man with greater self-efficacy is likely to be more effective, even if both men start with the same expectations, inspiration, control and willpower.

Another big name in research into SRT, Barry Zimmerman, put forth his own self-regulated theory: self-regulated theory of learning.

Self-regulated learning (SRL) relates to the method of making a student assume accountability for their own learning and leading to academic achievement (Zimmerman, 2002).

This process takes place in three steps:

1. Planning: the student plans his / her mission, sets objectives, describes the battling strategies and/or establishes a timetable for the assignment;

2. Monitoring: the student puts its plans into action at this point and strongly tracks its success and practice with the approaches it has chosen;

3. Reflecting: at last, the student's response to how she accomplished that and why she did it the

way she did after the task is complete and the grades are in.

Students gain deeper insights into how they think, what behaviors work best for them, and eventually perform at a higher level, through taking the initiative and controlling their own learning. This development stems from the multiple learning opportunities at each stage:

1. Students have the opportunity to focus on their self-assessment during the planning phase, and learn how to choose the best success strategies;

2. Students get the experience during the monitoring phase of implementing the strategies they have selected and making real-time changes to their plans if necessary;

3. Students synthesize everything they have experienced and commented on their perceptions during the reflection phase, discovering what is right for them and what to alter.

The Self-Regulatory System

Considering the self-regulatory mechanism may be useful for deeper comprehension of SRT. While the paradigm is unique to self-regulation relating to health and illness (rather than emotional), the complex processes at work during self-regulation of any kind remain a good example.

Leventhal's Self-Regulatory Mechanism adapted from Hagger and Orbell (2003) explains how the method works: stimuli are presented (i.e. anything happens that causes a reaction, if it's an idea, anything stated by another human, having important news, etc.); the participant has meaning of the stimulus, both cognitively (understanding) and emotionally (feeling);

Self-control and self-regulation

If you believe there's something in common with self-control and self-regulation, you are right. They are similar concepts and they're working with some of the same methods. And they remain two separate systems.

Self-control is about inhibiting strong urges; self-regulation is about reducing the frequency and strength of severe actions by controlling stress-load and rehabilitation. Indeed, self-regulation is what renders self-control feasible, even impossible in certain ways. "In this way, we may think about self-regulation as a more unconscious and involuntary mechanism (unless the person decides to consciously regulate or change his or her self-regulation), whereas self-control is a series about purposeful decisions and behaviors.

Understanding reduced Ego

One essential principle of SRT is self-regulatory depletion, also called ego depletion.

This is a condition in which an individual's motivation and influence of self-regulation mechanisms has been used up, and the resources available to suppress desires has been wasted, sometimes contributing to weak decision-making and performance (Baumeister, 2014).

When a human is faced with many temptations (especially strong temptations), when it comes to controlling desires, he or she must expend an equally powerful amount of energy for this reason. SRT claims that for this purpose people have a small will, and once it is gone two things happen:

1. Inhibitions and behavioral constraints are lower, indicating the individual is less driven and less likely to resist temptations;

2. Temptations, desires, or impulses are felt even more intensely while the will is at a regular, undepleted stage (Baumeister, 2014).

In SRT, that's a crucial point. It explains that we fail to resist participating in "poor behavior" while we're attracted by it for a long period. It shows, for example, that certain dieters will hold a tight diet all day, yet when they're attracted by food, they'll give in until they're getting dinner.

It also explains that a married or otherwise engaged couple may resist an offer from someone who hasn't been their girlfriend for days or weeks yet who will ultimately give in and have an affair.

Recent research in neuroscience supports this notion of self-regulatory depletion. A 2013 study by Wagner and colleagues used functional neuroimaging to show that individuals who had drained their self-regulatory capacity experienced reduced interaction between brain regions involved in self-control and rewards.

Examples of self-regulatory actions why self-regulatory exhaustion is a daunting challenge, SRT does not mean that it is unlikely to stay in charge of your impulses and activities while your capacity is exhausted. It simply notes that when your energy level decreases it gets harder and harder.

However, there are several instances of effective self-regulatory conduct, including though the person is uncertain regarding appropriate self-regulation.

Examples are:

- A cashier who will be polite and calm when he is approached by an angry customer for the item which he has little power over;
- A child who refrains from throwing a tantrum when it's said she can't have the gift she likes with eagerness;
- A people who are fighting over something that's significant for both of them to try to take some time and calm off before they resume their conversation.
- As you can see, self-regulation encompasses a wide range of activities from minute-to - minute actions to broader, more meaningful decisions that can impact significantly on whether we are achieving our goals.

Balancing Ego with Emotional Intelligence

Much of my leadership preparation curriculum centered on the influence of the Ego of Leaders. At the flip hand, the ego will give tremendous trust, motivation and endurance in holding organizations raising the bar. The ego can be a dominant and damaging influence on job success, while the opposite side can't. I realize, as I witnessed with many clients this out of reach personality firsthand.

At the other side, mental intelligence or EQ provides an outstanding match for the ego.

Jen Shirkani's fantastic book, "Ego vs. EQ: Why Top Leaders Conquer 8 Ego Traps with Emotional Intelligence" is published. She discusses the implications with an overweight ego. She observed that more than one-third of all CEOs struggle on the job during their first 18 months. A further analysis undertaken by Harvard Business Review showed a 1/3 of Fortune 500 Enterprises CEOs did not make it beyond 3 years.

'Self-Importance' is another form of talking of the Ego. The vital components of leadership are having an inner trust, being aware of skills and abilities, and high self-worth.

Yet this is how, in our lives, an out of balance ego works out:

- The Correct Option. There's typically the apprehension of letting go or any other vulnerability at stake here. Opening out for anything. We debate to the full end. To tell white lies. The signs are typically being aggressive.
- Further emphasis on our Reputation. Worried on how we behave at others. Focusing about how successful we are in many people's minds, about our accomplishments and our expertise. Particularly for those we find essential to us.
- Paranoid in the making. Believing other individuals is out to kill them. Mini 'turf-wars' formation. Am hunting for partners. Disputing legitimacy between others.

She defines 8 'Ego Traps' in the Book of Shirkani. I've definitely encountered three specific ones with the coaching executives here:

- Ignoring some suggestions you don't need. ("If they don't like it here, they might get a position somewhere" thought)

- Underestimate how many eyes are monitoring you. (And being unselfish about your impact).
- Perding front-line touch. (To say other individuals will get the work done).

And what would you do if you accept that your ego is out of control?

Let's switch to Relational Intelligence. EQ has been shown to be more effective than IQ and can be learned. Three really important tactics are in here.

1) Self-Consciousness.

Understanding yourself is the foundation of EQ. This respects your abilities and shortcomings, holds your feelings in control and recognizes your influence most importantly. How do you feel? When were you last asking for feedback? Where do you have the most respect? Where the blind spots are?

2) Others Write

The second main aspect of EQ in leadership connection is the capacity to correctly interpret individuals and circumstances. High-EQ leaders appreciate their people, know how to bring the most out of them and see their value.

3) May communicate with someone, emotionally.

EQ's third element is being able to establish good partnerships. It spends time and money in the company as well as the personal facets of the partnership. Successful leaders will overlook past errors, resolve minor resentments, and offer credit and recognition where it is deserved.

Steps Next?

My advice will be as follows:

• Self-audit-when the self is out of control? Taking a good and honest look at how the ego conducts itself.

• An EQ self-evaluation-consider the talents and weak points in emotional intelligence. Recognize where you might exploit your abilities, and where your feelings would need to stay under check.

Why self-regulation is key to growth

Remember how self-regulation allows one to develop and sustain a balanced sense of well-being.

Overall, plenty of data indicate that those who demonstrate self-regulation effectively experience better well-being in their regular life. Researchers Skowron, Holmes, and Sabatelli (2003) find a significant correlation between better self-regulation and wellbeing for both men and women.

The findings are comparable for adolescent studies. A 2016 survey found that adolescents who consistently partake in self-regulatory activities experience greater well-being than their peers, including enhanced personal fulfillment, perceived social encouragement, and the effect of happiness (i.e. positive feelings)

Moreover, those who ignored their emotions rather than facing them head-on suffered poorer well-being, like greater depression, more harmful consequences (i.e., weak emotions), and worse overall psychological wellbeing (Verzeletti, Zammuner, Galli, Agnoli, & Duregger, 2016).

Knowledge and social stability

To become more concrete, one of the aspects in which self-regulation leads to well-being is through emotional intelligence. Self-regulation, or the extent to which a person may regulate or manage his or her feelings and desires, is an important piece of emotional intelligence and it is simple to see why: Can you picture someone with a high level of self-awareness, motivation and social skiing?

There is something different about that image because of the essential role of self-regulation in emotional intelligence. But emotional intelligence, as researchers Di Fabio have yet discovered Kenny, is closely related to well-being (2016).

The more we understand and address our emotions and the emotions of others, the more we make sense of our circumstances, respond to them and achieve our goals (Ackerman, 2019).

Social skills

People with strong social skills are typically team players. Besides concentrating on their own performance, they help others grow and flourish. They can handle conflicts, they are outstanding networkers, and they improve the building and maintaining partnerships.

CHAPTER 4

Secrets for Developing High Social Emotional Intelligence

A lthough our culture naturally stresses knowledge that is more tangible and visible (good grades), our ability to conduct oneself in social situations is the one that goes largely unnoticed and neglected. Our main key to success is the ability of controlling our emotions in social environments, as well as being able to understand the thoughts of others. While everyone works hard on their book smarts, social smarts are critical as well and tend to be more important than the intelligence quotient in reality.

Take for example a situation in which you are questioning two leadership candidates. Joanne is somewhat more qualified, more skilled and more experienced than Rose. Rose does have the ability to understand others, work as a team member, though, and she can even inspire and motivate a team to achieve higher goals. Joanne is highly skilled in technical matters but not very good at understanding and managing the emotions of the people.

How are you planning to employ as Recruiting Manager?

Evidently Rose. In today's culture, the opportunity to perceive and express the feelings of people in the best possible manner is an invaluable asset.

Our capacity to develop connections and work out our way across social settings is Emotional Intelligence (SI).

Here are few well established gems that will boost your social-emotional knowledge by:

Adopt & Change

Don't suffer with the tendency to constantly mimic the situation of another human. Humans are designed to mimic the thoughts and desires of those around us. This is part of empathy! Of course we know what others experience. Even though, we also seek the middle path and strive to struggle off this sense of mirroring the feelings of the other individual. Say your partner gets angry and yells at you, for example. You feel they're nuts.

Nevertheless, you have read how necessary it is to pacify the condition by not responding similarly. You decide to remain quiet. You then attempt to quiet your companion down. It is here where further trouble starts. The frustrated person thinks 'you don't get them,' 'you don't get what they're attempting to suggest,' or 'you're never seeing them.' You have wanted to pacify the already tense scenario, throughout your opinion. How did the fire backfire?

This is because, at times, instead of listening to the other person's thoughts, we want to take the easy path to battle that reflects their feelings. Place yourself where your companion is and carry on his or her mental state of mind instead. This will help you get a clear insight about how they behave. It also allows them to realize you appreciate where they come from, rendering the circumstance less unfriendly.

Be assertive, not violent

Learning to be more assertive without being hostile is one of the benefits of being socially intelligent. People who are assertive know how to not only please people without insulting them.

Assertiveness is a prudent and sincere representation of views and emotions. "This weekend I would just like to go to the match." This is a positive comment.

Without being aggressive or demanding you make your needs clear. Aggressiveness is characterized by a strong lack of regard for other people's interests and privileges. When you're violent, you're just looking at it from an egoistic angle, just attempting to achieve a self-fulfilling purpose. The aggressive version of the above statement would be: "We're good this weekend for the games."

You express the argument just like a judgment on the other party without consideration or care.

On the other hand, assertiveness is characterized by respect and understanding for the feelings or opinions of the other person, even if you may not agree with that. Although violent says, "Only I am correct," assertive says, "I value it while your view does not align with mine. We should choose to disagree with that.'

Assertive citizens don't let anyone take advantage of them and recognize when without being stern to draw the line. They know when to tell someone 'no' without harming their feelings. If you express love for an individual or community of people, the pain can lessen. Be assertive, while showing respect, makes your stand clear.

However, anytime you demonstrate a lack of respect or empathy for the feelings, opinions or wishes of the other individual, you tread violence. Assertive persons are not willing to fight by their beliefs. They're not shying away from voicing their needs and objectives to others. Assertive people regard others as partners and work from mutual respect point of view. They have no intention of hurting others, except themselves. There are the individuals who strive for a win-win scenario all the time.

Aggressive people have a deep desire to win and operate from a point where they disrespect or overlook the needs of others. They see harming or disrespecting others as a by-product to achieve or prosper. Instead of arriving at a win-win solution, aggressive folks focus more on proving themselves right. They mastered the art of playing upon the insecurities and fears of other individuals.

Social and emotional intelligence is about being assertive and accepting the needs and views of other individuals while expounding your own needs and opinions. As a chief, one has to be assertive about making oneself known while still having respect and empathy for the team. And if you don't agree with someone, you have to try to figure out where they come from to improve your social-emotional quotient along with your social abilities.

Here are a few strategies to improve your assertiveness:

• Maintain true and transparent contact

Listen actively to the thoughts, desires, emotions and expectations of the other person. Keep an eye on verbal and non-verbal cues to better understand them. Not listening to response or respond, listening to learn. Similarly listen to the other party without interrupting.

Before you plunge in with your analysis, let them finish what they mean!

• Be not guilty

Don't feel guilty for rejecting anyone if they don't match in with your stuff system. Listen to people at the same time, without making them feel bad for communicating their needs.

• Stay cool and controlled

Maintain eye contact even in a stressful or possibly unpleasant scenario, maintain a calm smile and talk with a clear, gentle tone. People who are assertive seldom allow their feelings affect their acts. They have a firm handle on themselves and even in the most difficult circumstances, can keep calm.

• Practice assertiveness before a mirror

Pretend to communicate with a companion who encourages you to do something you don't want to do. How are you going to express that to them freely and honestly? Concentrate on your sentences, body language, gestures, speech and sound.

• Always consider citizens as friends and not rivals

Think teamwork in the office environment, and not rivalry.

• Adhere to statements using 'I'

Instead of thinking, "We shouldn't go there," for example, strive to suggest, "I don't think we should go there." It helps you remain strong, without being pushy. You express your thoughts without having a summons which demonstrates respect for the other person.

•Stay patient

It won't arrive immediately, if you're not an assertive guy. Enable yourself to be more aware of the verbal and non-verbal interactions when communicating to others to display more assertiveness.

• Value different views

Realize that when someone doesn't share the same view as you, it doesn't mean it he or she is incorrect or incorrect. Choose to disagree with others and empathize with them even though you don't approve. Try to find out where they come from and what pushes them to act the way they do.

Instead of proving your point or being concerned with competing, try to hold a win-win, problem-solution approach. Do not treat the other party as an adversary during circumstances when you're in disagreement with another human. Concentrate now for a win-win approach that would fix the problem with those concerned.

Practice empathy

Empathy is the ability to put oneself in the hands of someone else and sense their emotions or feelings just as they perceive it. It is the ability to understand and feel the emotions of other people, as if they occurred to you. Predictably, in today's world the ability to experience the emotions of other people and use this experience to help others feel better about the situation is a much sought-after talent.

Empathy is an essential element of social-emotional intelligence. You will reach out to them by empathizing with them, to manage their emotions more effectively. The capacity to recognize how somebody thinks can be used to motivate, inspire, drive and positively influence others.

Here are the main keys to cultivate greater empathy:

Traveling regularly to experience different countries, communities, habits and values is a perfect way for people whose lives are different from yours to develop empathy and appreciation. You will develop a better understanding and appreciation of people other than you. There will be a greater understanding of why they are behaving and acting the way they are doing.

Look at the overt and covert prejudices. Most of us work with specific biases based on ethnicity, gender, age, education, occupation, etc. When it comes to empathizing or listening to people they behave as a barrier. Make a list of prejudices you believe you have, and try to read views that go against your biases. Look for evidence that tests the assumptions and try to overcome certain prejudices steadily.

Nurture a productive curiosity. You can learn something from an 'inexperienced subordinate,' a 'picky client,' or a 'hotheaded boss.' Rather than labeling people, develop a sense of curiosity about what you can genuinely learn from them. This will give the people around you a better understanding and appreciation.

Volunteer in your free time at an NGO or charity organization. It will not only help you appreciate what you already have but will also facilitate greater empathy for people who aren't as fortunate as you. The knowledge that you made a positive impact on someone's life will make you feel better about yourself. When you spend time with the less fortunate, you develop the ability to understand other people's challenges and problems, which in turn boosts your empathy factor.

During situations where there is a conflict because of a difference in opinion, a resolution becomes easier when you understand the other party's underlying fears, needs, and motivations. You'll understand why even when they're negative towards you. Watch debates (especially during elections) to consider different viewpoints and understand why people believe their way of doing things. If you find yourself tilting in one direction, search immediately for proof that goes against your stance. This will help you develop the ability to appreciate multiple viewpoints without your stand being dogmatic. Empathy in its essence is about developing a greater understanding of the point of view or situation of another person, even when you don't necessarily agree with them.

Predict how a person will act or react in a given situation by putting yourself in their shoes. This will give you a greater understanding and perception of how people feel about any given situation.

Be fully present by keeping away your phone, turning off your email alerts, and mindfully listening to the other person. According to the research conducted by a professor at UCLA, things we speak make up for only seven percent of the message we are trying to communicate. The other 93 percent is determined by our body language and tone of voice. You are missing important clues if you aren't fully focusing on the other person while communicating with them.

They may be saying something that is contrary to what they feel, which you will miss if you are too preoccupied to focus on their non-verbal signals.

Smiles are infectious. Rarely does someone smile at you, and in return you don't smile. It's the best way to connect and show solidarity or concern for others. A simple smile can boost the brain's feel-good hormones and stimulate its reward centers. By laughing, you will do a whole lot of good for yourself and everyone.

Address people by name, and publicly praise them. What is it you've heard about publicly praising and admonishing people in private? Effective leaders have mastered the art of using the names of people while addressing them and using more encouraging declarations. Highlighting their skills or accomplishments in public makes each person feel important. That inspires them to work even better. Even if a person's success slips, keep openly pointing to milestones to inform them of their true potential. People respond to praise with wonder.

And give people unique feedback. As you learn to be more specific while appreciating people, your empathy and social-emotional quotient will increase. For example, instead of saying, "You did a good job," tell someone, "Despite the fact that the topic was complex and extensive, the project was very well-researched and thorough," or, "Do you want to share the inspiration behind your brilliant concept of sales growth? Be a champion at listening.

We've seen how hearing is intrinsic to the assertiveness and empathy process, both of which are vital to boosting your social-emotional quotient.

Listening isn't just about hearing what people say.

It's also figuring out what they're leaving untold through their body language, voice, emotions and word choice. Let us consider an example to understand better how listening (or tuning in to verbal and non-verbal patterns) is central to the communication process. It's Friday evening, and everybody is getting ready to let their hair down through the weekend after a hectic week at work.

They shut down their computers and get ready to leave when the CEO of the company, Sue, walks in and informs them that two weeks ahead pushes the deadline for the project they have worked so hard on. Naturally everyone is frustrated and stressed out.

The manager of the project remains at her desk nervously contemplating how to meet the deadline. Ann, the project manager, says, "We're still going to do a good job and submit the project according to the new deadline." Another employee, Dan, is getting to work on his computer, and few people are leaving. Many team members claim they can accommodate these new adjustments. Sue leaves the office realizing it's going way better than she expected. What she didn't catch was the incoherence in the project manager's body language and words, who left the office in a rage while responding to an email from a prospective recruiter.

Other members of the team went to grab a coffee and were almost in tears because of the newfound stress they face. Yeah, nobody told Sue how they were actually feeling as she called for input.

So how she was supposed to know how they really feel about pressing the deadline? Do you believe she was responsible in any way for not knowing the emotions of her employees? She wasn't really attentive or tuned in to what they were trying to convey. She went along with their terms but didn't catch what they left unsaid. A large part of social-emotional intelligence is knowing what people are leaving unsaid. Here are some suggestions for improving excellent listening abilities:

Be open minded. Do not work with a preconditioned or prejudiced mentality and be more open to listening without identifying or criticizing people. One of the major challenges in the communication process I would claim is listening to people without jumping to conclusions. Don't try to hijack your conversation, or try to finish your sentences. Remember, the person is communicating their ideas, thoughts, opinions, and feelings. Let them freely express themselves without being interrupted. We often spend more time planning what we are going to say in response to something rather than actively listening to a person to understand them.

Don't listen to respond. Listen to understand what the person is trying to convey. Focus completely on what the speaker is saying rather than rehearsing your responses. Even if it seems uninteresting, listen. Wait for the speaker to stop or clarify doubts before asking questions.

Don't interrupt someone in their speech midway through. Hold your questions, instead, until they pause. "Let us take a few seconds back. I didn't really understand what you meant by XYZ. "Occasionally our inquiries will throw people in a completely different direction from where they want to take the conversation. If the speaker heads in a different direction, bring them back to the original subject by asking something like," It was great information of ABC, but tell us more about XYZ right now.

CHAPTER 5

Controlling Emotions

Social
Skills

Emotions are one of the driving forces within the life of all. We all have them and they saw us through many things, regardless of who we are or how old we are. They were there when we passed through crushing and traumatic heartbreaks, when some of our biggest fears were confronted and overcome, and when we needed the encouragement to walk away from toxic circumstances. They are not only there during the bad times, of course. They gave us the ability to experience the joys of true friendship, affection for each other and one of them all's strongest feelings, to love as profoundly as we can.

Allowing emotions to lead the way is simple, especially when one considers how strong and powerful they can be, but with reason and logic these feelings should always be balanced. That seems to be a daunting thing to worry about, isn't it? Emotional management is uncommonly heard about.

That being said, emotional control is a term that I have heard a lot in my whole life. Particularly my mum was the one who told me about EQ. It was something that I sometimes lost sight of as an intuition, by becoming so deeply engaged and/or active. As a consequence, when I should have controlled them I often let my emotions rule over me. What is EQ, then?

Everybody knows what IQ is, right? Ok, EQ is basically the equivalent to desire, becoming our emotional intelligence. Identifying and reinforcing the EQ helps us control our emotions. It's the capacity not only to understand our own feelings but others' emotions. We know empathies are extremely strong at sensing other people's emotions, but they aren't really successful at knowing the difference between certain feelings and calling them appropriately, as well as distinguishing their own emotions from others' emotions. That's why developing and understanding EQ is important, because you can use these emotions and feelings as a guide to manage and/or adjust emotions. Once you've learned to manage them, you'll be better equipped to respond to situations, achieve your goals, and in any given situation behave / think more accordingly.

Having a good level of control over your feelings doesn't mean you can't fall in love head over heels or you can't get a little bit of a mental breakdown every now and then. After all we are all people. These encounters are completely natural to go through. That said, there are some feelings that lead one to lose a little amount of rationality and critical thought, such as envy and rage. Here's where understanding how to cope with such unpleasant feelings falls in. If we don't treat them properly, they could spin out of reach and drag us down a pit of misery further down.

And how can we get better physically to stop catastrophe? I'll run over a variety of tips below for how to achieve just that. These techniques can also help you become better emotionally than ever before.

Using Body Language

Body language is the nonverbal, symbolic form of communication by body movements, facial expressions, and gestures. Our body language is typically a series of involuntary acts that represent our internal response to various circumstances. As with actual language, the manner in which we walk will teach others how we feel and what we think, just as we can understand what others feel and think depending on their action.

It's crucial how you interact through movement and gesture. Often you will offer away the real feelings and desires more frankly than a physical response would and in certain cases we really don't really intend to respond. The physical action is normal. We don't need to care over the movements we create. The reason we raise our eyebrows is not something we suggest it in advance.

Understanding the body language is what allows it easier for us to understand how others are listening to us and behaving towards us. If you ever noticed someone wandering around continuously or getting quickly disturbed during a conversation? They really don't seem very curious about what you've got to say, do they? Are there other moments during an active discussion that you can hold your eye contact so long that you fail to blink? There's no "right" way to use body language, but you can show more positive reactions and even render yourself more available by being more flexible and comfortable in yourself and with the motions of the body. Take posture as another example; you are more inclined to stress while you are nervous in a social setting. You should keep your head up high as you loosen your shoulders to look more relaxed. These basic movements will offer off the impression that you are more at ease at that point in time, even though you feel discomfort.

Being mindful of your own actions and expressions is a good way to try to hold the feelings concealed and under balance. Of course, having stuff locked up is not healthy, but as an intuition, in some cases, you do not want the large load of thoughts and emotions to spill out. Stay strong and hold your head high. You realize as well as I do that these unpleasant feelings are transient. If you don't let them get to you, and don't let people realize they're getting to you, you'll notice that at the end of the day they're simpler to free.

And too much detrimental emotion around the environment, Constructive thought is also impossible to do.

Healthy thought continues with self-conversation. Self-talk is easily recognizable enough. That is the sound that the word plays on a regular basis in all of our heads and the endless sequence of thinking. Unfortunately, if you spend so long trapped within your own mind, those feelings are susceptible to depression and will drive you down the road of pessimism. This road is full of self-doubt and uncertainty that clearly doesn't require a compassionate empathy — or someone for that matter — in their lives. So now we could transform the word into a constructive one. Aching yourself to have optimistic feelings is great for your mental health; it will lower levels of depression and enable you to deal with challenging conditions. The mental training takes time, though, because it always takes time to break every old habit.

Try to appreciate and look for humor during the day to make your mood lighter. Throughout the day, be patient and reasonable with yourself by assessing what you truly believe, and deciding whether it is good or bad. From taking a deep breath each time you hear those feelings. Question whether they are appropriate or not, or true. If not, transform them into a new road. You might want to try meditation as it is a great way to train the mind to let go of emotions, handling them like clouds floating across the sky. You take note of these, but then you let them slip by because there's no other option. Surround yourself with people who are optimistic and compassionate. Forgetting and letting go of the negative feelings in company of good friends who make you chuckle more than anything else is far better.

Know that if you work hard enough something will have a good spin on it. This can only help your mental wellbeing, after all. Positivity doesn't disregard the challenges of life; it takes certain concerns and transforms them around in order to make the most of a difficult circumstance.

You could drop the birthday cake at a big party, but just because you ruined the pretty icing doesn't mean it's inedible. It could be a story that you gaze with a grin back at. All this depends on how you react to the scenario.

Positive Talks

Words are one of the world's most powerful powers, and are performed by one of the human body's smallest organs. We don't all know that, but it does have an impact over everything we say out into the universe. Subconsciously we are watching what we are seeing. Conscious of what you are bringing into the world; does it affect your life favorably or negatively?

It just creates more harmful energies as you act negatively, which may cause anxiety which hopelessness. It will also intensify distress and other emotional disorders including stress and fear. Note, your mental wellbeing is of immense significance, and is strongly linked to your physical wellness.

People will only judge you by the way you talk but also by the way you communicate to yourself and others. We were always in positions where we were either gossiped or judged too unfairly. These circumstances may be quickly overlooked but they can affect us much of the time.

Although these awful phrases and assumptions may have a big effect on us, there's almost as much influence of constructive speech. We can express compassion through it, our care for each other, and provide reassurance when it's most important.

Words are also a way of expressing the mental exhaustion, and just reflecting about how you feel can be one of the best relievers of tension. Having said that, you need to be conscious that moaning all the time is harmful. Just like with positive thinking, you get to choose how to look at your situation. If you continually whine, you will be seen by people as an individual who constantly complains. But if you're trying to say something positive any time you talk to someone, they're going to remember that about you and so are you going to.

Consider your potential voice, and note that constructive speaking will definitely affect your emotions. Adjust your voice sound if need be. Let others know how you feel and represent who you are and use your expression. If you wish to be a better guy, so it is up to you to do so. And if you want to unleash the frustration that keeps you down, you should use exercise to do so.

Create Your Own Personal Space

Is there a certain space that you love, a place where you can go and think about all your thoughts and feelings, and feel safe and secure? It may get curled up in bed, or a spot in your favorite coffee shop, or a quiet corner in your local library. There are many opportunities. When we talk about or mention our own personal space that is the type of image that comes to mind. Your room is that place of comfort and enjoyment that belongs to you and only you, the one you may have first thought of. In this situation, though, such a room is far more complicated than a mere adored spot.

Your own personal space is one you set limits on. You can decide what's going on and what's not going on. We set limits for protecting ourselves physically as well as emotionally. It is our own comfort zone where, whether during a physical or emotional interaction, we can keep things at a distance. The act of breaching a barrier within this room can be anything that makes you uncomfortable in any way, if it's someone who's too busy around you when you don't like loud noise, anyone seated too near to you, or even a partner or friend that needs you to disclose anything intimate that you're not willing to share. It's important to set and adhere to those boundaries. Any problems concerning them should be treated with care and seriousness, instead of being shrugged off.

You might feel drained, agitated or upset with yourself for being angry and/or hurt when your personal space is compromised. You may not even know why you react like this, especially if you haven't identified what your boundaries are. Because of that basic reality, your self-esteem can fall, which can harm your trust. Border crossing is a form of violation. Few situations can be more extreme than others, but no matter how large or tiny the limits can stay the same. Defining them out for yourself is critical.

We all have different personal spatial needs and ideas. It's important to note that making your own is good. It is also intimate, and to want that is perfectly good. Never feel guilty for maybe having more space than anyone. What's essential is that you understand that you need it. And we all are. Be transparent, strong and respectful when describing to people what your personal space is. Hopefully they'll value you sufficiently for them to agree. It is generally safer to pass on from the individual and the case under any situations where this does not happen. It does not warrant your lovely self to be disrespected in this way.

First of all that appreciation begins with yourself. Value yourself enough not to give in to anxiety. To not encourage others to exploit us takes a lot of self-respect.

Work on Time Management

In our fast-paced lives time management is crucial. If we are not trying to control our time properly, we will be adversely affecting our feelings. A definition of that is exhausting oneself and overworking ourselves, which can trigger a storm of depression. We are making an effort to avoid this toxicity.

Today, some of us work best under pressure — which, to be frank, is not the best option — while others are more likely to start long in advance of their workload. We're both vulnerable to burning out in whatever manner you choose to function. If we don't take care of ourselves well, our resources and the amount of work that we are burdening ourselves with, we will suffer from that. Believe me it's not fun burnout. If you've never seen that, be grateful and do your utmost to never get there. If you do, you will realize you will never want to do it again.

When you think about it, time management really is important. Without this our lives cannot function properly. We'd be late for meetings, behind for jobs and, to say the least, behind on payments. So how should we do it correctly?

Hold your mind focused, just concentrate on the work. Don't run down.

Evite tension, whenever feasible. That all seems fairly easy, isn't it?

If we could just avoid stress now of course, we will. Stress normally allows our bodies and minds to easily become weary, making us seem a bit darker than normal. If our body is a mess our head will feel the same way, and our feelings will feel that way too. It is better to take breaks, above all else. Often we all need a rest. That doesn't say you're going to push yourself to a break point and then take time off. No, you just require small breaks in between. This may be an easy, daily break when operating to assist with those limited attention times. Make a cup of tea, close your eyes for five minutes, and maybe do some respiratory exercises.

Ultimately it's really about figuring out what works best for you. Good time management is a constant and ongoing activity. Learn to focus all the mental draining and burden on yourself beforehand. During those small breaks you can even focus on these. If you work them in your daily schedule, you can feel the stress that you are feeling at the thought of a break start to slip away. In your life it is all about living and leisure. We urgently need our bodies to heal. Devoting attention to our physical and mental support will avoid burning out.

Other methods of controlling emotions

Life is tough on the whole, not just for empathy. Here people are hurting. It's so tempting, as an ego, to believe that you're the only one feeling emotional pain. But always realize that most people are out in a miserable country. We run into various things in our day-to-day lives and make our lives difficult. We should learn about new strategies instead of giving up, in order to improve the quality of our lives.

Empathic life is marked by emotional instability. They have to gain a certain level of control of their feelings for an intimacy to lead a normal life. In reducing emotional and mental pain and having an empathy lead a fulfilling life, the following tips are key.

Exercising

It is remarkable at times how easy the solution for our troubles can be. If you are already really depressed, you need not take your credit card and buy any expensive drugs whose side effects are uncertain. All you have to do is wear on training shoes and go out into the gym or arena. Do intense workouts or sprint sessions. The burden you faced earlier is going to go away. Exercising will not only relieve stress but also improve the brain health, skin health and immunity.

Start a journal

Writing down our mental and emotional experiences helps to alleviate us from tension. Those who maintain a journal and write down any event in their life are far more likely than people who don't maintain a journal to have positive feelings. A journal will also help you find out who you really are. Over time, you'll get to observe your actions and identify the patterns.

Make routine

Buffalos and elephants, as they like, get up and spend their day. But we are people. We have to have a schedule or else we are going to pay a big amount. When you have a routine it means that you know how to spend every moment. If you don't have a routine, choices will likely overwhelm you, and make the poor choice anyway. It costs nothing to think through what your average is like, or rather what it should be like, and then to come up with a routine that will guide you through the day.

Spend some time with your friends and relatives

Sometimes we underestimate the need for good relations to our emotional health. When we are surrounded by our blood relationships we tend to be genuinely happy. We tend to be happy too when our friends surround us. So if you're going through a stressful moment, the answer is simply to look for contact with your family or friend, and they're going to regain their emotional balance.

Be an early riser

If you sleep like an old lion, then you will obviously have problems. You get to condition your mind for the day ahead when you are an early riser, and work towards achieving your important goals. Rising up early will give you a head start and you are likely to run into more opportunities as opposed to waking up later in the day. Early risers will handle the heavy tasks and scatter the easy tasks throughout the remainder of the day, reducing mental distress as a result.

Treat yourself to a workout every day

Maybe the explanation you most often feel sad is because you don't feel like a leader or a survivor. One of the ways to overcome this feeling of inadequacy is through creating a daily challenge for yourself. You should push yourself to raise something, make some money, reach out to people to find out about their day, and so on. Essentially, it's about making your emotional health improved and constantly challenging yourself.

Man up to the truth

It does not matter what's happening right now in your world. It doesn't matter what you've missed, or what obstacles you encounter. But if you muster the courage to face your truth, and seek solutions to your dilemma, it will give you a world of success. Any people who aren't bold enough will resort to addictions and vices to hide from their life. But the effect is that their situation actually gets worse. If you can collect the courage to confront your issues, you've won half the battle.

Listen to calming songs

Music is soul food. Ensure that every now and then you listen to music to hold your spirits up. Often, listen to upbeat music to change your moods when you are facing a big stressful condition, or when you have lost confidence.

Take good care of yourself

It can be enticing when you go through emotional distress to shut yourself up and never venture outside again. But get rid of those feelings and start taking care of yourself tremendously. Take the time to prepare the recipes you like, buy the clothes that carry your charm out, and get yourself groomed to the heavens. Don't err in denying your wishes. It will help you develop a positive reputation while you take great care of yourself, and will prevent stress from entering your mind.

Relax

If you have emotional distress you need to rest in order to feel better for yourself. Overworking itself is one of the common reasons people feel worried over. But you'll restore your momentum when you take that well-deserved rest, and go back to being active again.

Meditation

It cannot be overstated how critical this practice is when it comes to getting rid of emotional and mental trauma. Meditation is a mental exercise which helps cleanse our mind and body of energy. Since the antiquity this activity has retained importance. You may practice meditation in different ways and each of them is intended for a particular purpose. A simple exercise in meditation involves finding a comfortable place, taking a calming posture, closing your eyes and then concentrating on your breath. Each breath you inhale and exhale can take away your fears, anxieties, and discomfort, and finally rejuvenate your sensation. The benefit about meditation is that you can practice it almost everywhere, except at your office. So whether you feel tired, burdened, or sad, all you have to do is meditate and you're going to be right again.

Discard obstacles

You will also get anxious because of the obstacles around you. These disturbances may arrive in the form of television, radio, and telephone. If you are searching for sleep or relaxing for example, these obstacles will discourage you from doing so. But, make sure you have them out.

Increase in concentration

Learn to improve your concentration and concentrate on your projects, and that's what's going to yield performance. If you struggle to prioritize, you'll still be short of your targets. Unmet objectives are among the main sources of depression. But if you're a champion, you're likely to develop a positive mindset, and it's going to make life enjoyable. One of the easiest ways to create energy is by becoming a beginner. For e.g., just throw yourself into work when you wake up at your office, as opposed to focusing on other problems.

Stop procrastinating

Procrastination is strongly connected to a lack of concentration. If you're a procrastinator, obviously you're performing a ton of disservices to yourself. Procrastination restrains you from achieving your essential goals in life. A procrastinator likes to push off stuff they need to have completed until tomorrow, and so tomorrow they continue the same pattern, then the day after tomorrow, because then they eventually run out of time, so that's then they start running stuff off, whilst some just give up because the job ahead is big then they don't have the time. Procrastination finishes terribly indefinitely.

Starter Exercises

Having an intuition is not something you can toggle on or off, it's just as much a part of you as your skin color. Although this ensures that you cannot switch off your talents, no matter how badly you might like to occasionally, there are steps that you can do to refresh yourself to ensure that your focus is balanced properly. The following methods all require time to learn, but once you can, you can notice that you can more effectively manage the pressure that comes with having an empathy.

You will note that these tasks are numbered as they represent the first phase in a 21-part curriculum designed to help you remove the negative side effects of your strength and also overloading the beneficial aspects to ensure you not only get as much out of your capacity as possible but also that you are able to help others around you as thoroughly as possible.

1. Break the cord:

This is an activity that you are likely to become very acquainted with through the years as it will help you avoid your energies from syphoning with others. You would inevitably come into touch with others when you develop partnerships in your everyday life, who sometimes unknowingly build bonds with you and pull your energy into themselves because it is such a good, caring energy. Even when these individuals have fallen out of your life, this depletion will occur, which suggests if you have never practiced this procedure then it is impossible to know how many directions the energy is going in.

To sever those etheric strings, what you need to do is start thinking about the people you've known in the past with whom you've had particularly deep or meaningful connections. Moving back over the years, one by one, and visualizing them as deeply as possible each time you run across one of these characters. Think, the stuff that you used to do together and the friendship that you formed before you said out loud, "I release you."

While there are definitely a variety of methods to cut the strings, this is a simple but effective way of cutting through those clinging on past their prime. You will need a more advanced method to eliminate those who don't want to be replaced, but with the above procedure, you'll be shocked at how much more energized you feel nearly right away. Once you've eliminated all of the remaining cords, you'll want to go through your memory inventory a few days a month to make sure there's no residual cords that need to be cut, keeping that up will make sure you have as much flexibility as you can for the most critical activities.

2. Place your aura straight:

It is perfectly natural, as a person, to understand the emotions that those around you are having, especially when they are particularly strong or unpleasant. Sadly, all these negative thoughts can also affect your own attitude, flooding the brain with passive, cynical, irrelevant or repeated thinking. When the emotions are good, they would automatically associate with positive vibrations that can contribute to regeneration, stability, and harmony; but, when pessimistic, they will lead to unhealthy blockages and unnecessary resistance levels.

Bad emotions are especially intrusive when they will calcify and vibrate inside you through the years in such a way that they catalyze a cascading reaction through your energy bodies whether they be physiological, physical, behavioral or spiritual. To guarantee these habits don't get an opportunity to grow up in a meaningful way, the first thing you'll want to do is look at your life to see if you're doing something, intentionally or unintentionally, to draw unpleasant individuals to circumstances to you. If you figure out this is the case, then it implies that you vibrate at the wrong level, normally without any active thinking on your side.

To re-center the energy field, you need to check for harmful feelings at the end of each day, then let them go. To do so, locate a nice room where you won't be disturbed for a few minutes before explaining to yourself what follows.

I have ownership over my body, my thoughts and my mind.

I am a converter, amplifier, and power generator. My motivation is used to achieve positive results

Throughout the process you'll want to reiterate these three statements to yourself over and over until it can pass through your head with very little active thought. In doing so, you'll probably want to imagine a silver white light suffusing the energy field and clearing it from any pollutants that may have stuck in it all day long. There is no set amount of time for this procedure, but you only need to go on until you believe like your aura appears to be self-correct. However, it is crucial not to panic, since doing so is a perfect way to keep unpleasant thoughts festering overnight by mistake.

3. Designate your own sacred space:

Every location in your home where you can let your mental walls down and really be at ease can be a sacred space. This can be something as complex as a specially created space for reflection, or just your workplace. Whatever it is, it should be a room solely yours, while some would definitely be able to come and go during the day's normal course. The room doesn't have to be huge or even indoors as long as it's a spot where you don't feel the need to be continuously on your guard against other people's unwanted thoughts.

You will also want to set aside at least 30 minutes a day so that you can spend it alone in that room. If your current living arrangements do not make this possible, then you may find success in creating a private mental space instead. While it might sound stupid, it can be extremely revitalizing even to set aside just 15 minutes to spend in your sacred mental space. It's best to start with a place you're familiar with when building your mental sacred space, as the clearer your mental image is of space, the more successful the exercise will be. Take the time to really focus down what the space looks like, how it feels, or whatever noises you may expect to hear, the stronger the more distinct.

4.   Smudge your energy field:

Smudging of your energy field is an excellent way to transmute extremely harmful energies away from your energy field. Although this isn't a strategy you ought to take out every day, you'll notice it's a perfect way to flush the physical, mental or emotional body emotions out of alignment.

Smudging is a kind of healing ritual that calls upon the spirits of holy plants in an attempt not just to push the harmful energies out of the body but also out of a physical room. You can think of it as having the same purpose as washing your hands before you eat.

Although the origins of the ritual date back to Native American Tradition, the concept of burning white sage together with other herbs for their medicinal results has a remarkable amount of science focused on it. Specifically, this burning emits toxic ions that research has specifically related to generally a more optimistic attitude. The aroma of sage specifically improves the supply of oxygen in the brain, resulting in natural decreasing tension. The smoke from some of the associated herbs literally reforms the chemical energy and air structure, resulting in a healing effect.

To effectively smudge, you must first focus yourself and make your motives plain in order to eliminate any of the negative from a particular room. You would also want to place the sage in a receptacle before setting them on fire and then gently blowing out the flame so the bowl stops smoldering. You may even light the end of a few leaves on fire if you like, and wave them by hand. Take a scoop of the smoke, and spill it over your heart, until the sage smokes well. Bear in mind your goal to clear your aura and then clearly put smoke over your ears, over your eyes and eventually over your third eye.

You may want to imagine yourself, when doing so, being filled by a warm, gentle light. Visualize the good energies rushing through the body when you breathe in. Enable each of the smudged areas to interact with the emotions you're having to draw and let the feeling of interconnectedness inspire you in general. If you smudge a room, make sure the smoke enters every inch of space to avoid negative energy pockets developing and darkening the whole space once again.

5. Connection to Nature:

For those who still feel exhausted by their talents, spending time in nature may offer a calming, restorative experience. Over all, this is just normal, since much of the unpleasant feelings you'll be coping with will be explicitly triggered by other individuals. As such, if you find you are unable to cope with the relentless flood of thoughts and feelings from others around you, a day or two spent in nature's isolation might be just what the doctor has ordered.

Spending time surrounded by nature can help anchor you and expel unnecessary emotions from your body whilst spending time with animals will offer a hard to beat form of calming energy therapy. Rolling barefoot helps you to consciously extract good energies from the earth. This method is known as relaxation and if you feel removed from the environment around you then this is a perfect way to try and reconnect.

6. Consider various stones:

Working with crystals and stones will make keeping focused on the present simpler for the empaths and not getting lost in a sea of thoughts and emotions. Obsidian is of special benefit in repelling toxic energies. Specifically, black obsidian is helpful when it comes to holding the auric field off depression or deliberately countering a direct spiritual assault. It's also helpful in holding you balanced when doing spiritual practice. It is also necessary to clean your stones the way you would your body as the harmful energies will build up inside them to render them a destructive force in your existence, rather than a productive one.

Make the most of it

You will be led through your first few steps of a spiritual journey in this part, which will help you flourish in your empathic abilities. Whatever kind of person you are, certain basic practices can always help to preserve your dynamic equilibrium and reinforce your sense of self. Pick and choose the methods that work better for you, or if necessary, integrate them all into your practice.

Objective Separation

Sadly, a significant percentage of empathies often begin to know their sensitivities as the empathy-deficient individuals, typically in early adulthood, leave them throughout their lives. Can characterize this phenomenon as an empathic judgment or rite of passage; others may define it as reaching the rock bottom until it ascends to enlightenment. When left behind, they eventually begin to realize the complexities of their unmet emotional needs, feeling alone, unspeakably exhausted or exploited, abused and undervalued. It's a difficult way to come to such a realization, but if you think you 're an empathy yourself, it may be prudent to adopt a constructive route, finding peace on your terms until you feel yourself unable and unable to do but.

Empaths appear to place their own interests above anyone else, and sometimes grow hectic, distracted teenage lives to excuse their erratic mood changes and irrational anxieties. If this is valid for you, then it may seem weird, undeserved or perhaps a little daunting to plan a substantial amount of alone time for yourself. Try to drive the apprehensions aside, and schedule a self-care vacation. Seek to plan an extended period — ideally a full day or longer — to clean your energy environment from all other people's waste, and get back in contact with yourself.

If money and time are no object so arranging a solo trip is a perfect way to do this. Water bodies, particularly the ocean, will provide an enormous amount of therapeutic energy to the empaths, rendering beaches and lakeshores excellent travel destinations. But be vigilant of big tourist spots, and note that many people are trying to avoid their problems, taking with them pain and destructive energies. With booze, caffeine surges, and other indulgences, they might be able to block out their own traumatic thoughts but it won't save you from picking up on their inner chaos. You will be best to skip the tourism sites and busy hours for this escape.

Camping is another perfect way to get in touch with nature when maintaining the inner balance. If protection is a concern for you, instead, you could schedule a few day hikes and spend secure nights in a hotel or travel car, behind locked doors. Yoga, yoga, and spa retreats, if you want more order in your holiday plans, often make fantastic destinations.

Of course, the expense of flying and the stresses of our jobs keep most of us from arranging a holiday at the drop of a hat, but there is still plenty you can do to reconnect with your root energies and find a balance in your home and community for two days alone. The point of this exercise is to interrupt the habit and isolate yourself from the fields of energy that often leak inside your own. You do not actually pay a lot of money to achieve so.

You'll want to limit screen time, interaction with colleagues, co-workers and loved ones, and addiction from alcohol or illicit substances to get the best out of this activity. If you're used to a busy lifestyle, you may want to prepare your own itinerary as an anxiety mitigating tactic. Or, if you feel ready for an extreme confrontation, leave the time free, begin with calm, reflective meditation and encourage your thoughts to cascade without limit. It may be an incredibly painful event, but there's no guilt about becoming exhausted, wanting to cut short the break, or reaching out for help to a loved one. Start noting, though, the pain is a part of development here. You may postpone the impact, or ease the hit, but you can't overwhelm it or indefinitely stop it. You are seeking your true selves through loneliness. Take that from an experience that's been through such a reckoning; the acute pain is worth the growth.

Meditation

Meditation represents a natural and rational next move to empathy. At first, sitting quietly, all alone with your thoughts can be quite uncomfortable. Try to remember that meditation has the purpose of letting those thoughts and emotions come, and then releasing them. Permit them to roll over you the way waves rush across your feet when you step along the seashore, washing up and then fading away easily, softly.

Often, you should meditate on specific subjects or issues you are struggling to understand. However, the purpose of meditation isn't to stir anxiety, so if you notice patterns of repetitive, obsessive, or negative thinking, you may want to change your approach before your next session.

If you already have a successful meditation practice, you might want to push yourself further and activate your third eye chakra by questioning your patterns of thought. Any spiritual guides recommend utilizing inquisition to assist this method, addressing each of your thoughts constantly with the question: "Is that true?" If that approach seems combative or causes emotions of internal conflict, instead you can exercise skepticism in your perceptions and entertain the possibility that the reality is the reverse of what you believe it to be.

Create safe haven

To ensure that self-care becomes a regular part of your new routine, throughout your life — literally, you'll want to make room for that. Even if it has to be inside a suitcase, make sure you find enough space to create your own sanctuary. You could think of it as a bubble of calm, a place for reflection, or a holy altar too. The idea is to create an ideal space where you can center yourself whenever life begins to feel overwhelming outside of this haven. Using candles and stones, smudge sticks, herbs, warm pillows, and blankets to cover it with. If you relish the endless potential of a blank slate, your haven might be completely bare, dark and quiet. There is no right or wrong path, just the one that feels good for you.

De-clutter and Organize your Living Space

Now that you've created a haven, your succeeding goal should be to organize the rest of your living space in a way that helps you to feel balanced, organized, reliable, and at peace. Even if you don't consider yourself a visual or materially-oriented person, the way your household looks matters; it is the first thing your eyes see every morning when you wake up, and last item you see before you fall asleep at night. His presence marks your visions and the inner realm as well as the mechanisms of your rational mind. In addition, it also has significance of the way it looks, tastes and looks.

If you think the feng shui ideas agree with you, then go ahead and review your home and furniture style, and rearrange everything you need to follow its values. This is specifically suggested for geomantic empaths — feng shui is often referred to as "geomancy," because it targets the same energy energies that are tailored to geomantic empathies.

If there is no time for a total interior redecoration project, then you may want to concentrate on removing excess energy from your living room instead. Take a mental list of exhibited objects in your house. How much of those were desire-based things you chose? How much of you needed out of necessity? Look out for the presents you've got and note that you're alone and nobody's criticizing you until you question yourself: how do I feel about the things I've been given? Will they have sentimental meaning and show a sense of attachment and caring for me? Or did any of them come from individuals who wanted to exploit or control my behaviors? Do any of these remind me that in my life, people don't see me or appreciate who I am?

If so, don't feel guilty to get it remembered. Gifts are often donated not from a position of kindness but in an effort to exercise willpower. Recognize these things as sources of harmful or residual energy in your household, and allow yourself to dispose of them, throw them away or submit them to remote storage.

Yoga, Tai Chi and the practice of physical mindfulness

There is no question that exercise is good for the body and the spirit, but when coupled with mindfulness it can be much more successful. Mindfulness is the idea of growing our knowledge of aspects we typically take for granted, or have grown to neglect, such as our habits of movement or thoughts. Yoga is highly common because it explores the need for physical balance and concentration, cultivating awareness, healing, acceptance, and self-love. It may also be conveniently adapted to meet several different desires, often entirely accepting the metaphysical aspect while at other occasions being concerned solely with the human body. You will quickly locate a yoga class to take, and there are plenty of yoga schools to choose from, based on the ability to improve strength, gain equilibrium, restore injury or experience deeper relief. You can also practice in your home alone, in nature, our outdoors.

Tai chi often promotes consciousness through a sequence of long, coordinated movement steps. Yoga will usually offer more of a physical task, whereas Tai chi takes a lot of concentration and attention so it tests the mind. It often seems more like a style of dance, so those who feel inspired by artistic expression can prefer tai chi to other related activities.

Grounding

Grounding is technically healthy but can only be as successful as the amount of energy that you will put through the exercise. Everything you need to do is remove your shoes and socks, position your feet on the earth (ideally in a location where you have a good bond with nature) and visualize your roots rising like a flower. Many empathies may shut their eyes, breathe deeply and during their grounding practice use a sort of mediation or affirmation.

One slogan that you might find useful is the alternating repetition of two phases: first, "I am one with the world," where you can replace the word "universe" with "all stuff" or the name of a higher power in your faith; and second, "I am separate, special, strong and purposeful." These two phrases express divided emotions that many empathies internally see back and forth between;

Any empathies find this phenomenon extremely strong in the proximity of coasts, historical structures or natural occurrences locations, such as volcanoes or earthquakes. For geomantic and precognitive empathies grounding is widely suggested.

Dietary changes

All living beings, whether plant, animal or person, are made of fire. So if you regularly consume foods that contain toxic energy sources, it may manifest in your body as physical discomfort, sickness, starvation, or even as an emotional effect, such as depression.

A diet for removal is an easy way to create a major difference in the energy sector, which typically induces dramatic improvement. You might be surprised to have aches or pain points erupted all of a sudden, even if you never considered them until they were flushed away.

Intermittent fasting may also be a helpful method for enhancing mental stability, but it can be performed carefully. This procedure may be unsafe for those who lead overly active lifestyles or suffer from dietary imbalances.

Exercises on affirmations and manifesting

Have you ever had the sense of getting stressed by a list of mental to-do, either putting it down on paper or asking someone else about it, then then remembering it's easy to do and not worth stressing?

Or, have you ever thought like a desire or vision was so far from entertainment — but then, announcing it loudly, you instantly found it pulled closer to you, fully within reach?

This is, in reality, a representation. The world listens to you whether you plan to fix it or not, but expressing your wishes and self-esteem directly will have a great ripple impact on your existence. It will improve your trust, enhance your determination, cultivate feelings of appreciation and help you retain positive attitude. Only make sure to express the reality without exaggeration, and be cautious not to challenge the world for something that you are unprepared to offer.

Use verbal or written affirmations to fuel inspiration, inspire self-love, and stay focused on your personal goals and values during any self-love exercise (yoga, reflection, swimming, or even while getting dressed in the morning, when you're pressed for time). Manifestation would concentrate mainly on the potential while affirmations can affect the present views of truth. Know that our emotions form our experiences, so the simple act of reframing negative thoughts through the expression of appreciation will shift the whole perspective on life.

Reporting

There is no right or incorrect approach to take advantage of this activity. Daily free-writing is a great opportunity to discover a better form of thinking, as well as to soothe unspoken tensions or fears. Any time you expect intrusion from a hypothetical cause of dissatisfaction in your energy sector, it can even be useful to read past articles from time to time, as a researcher. Journaling can help you detect positive and dangerous trends in your actions, both in your interpersonal relationships. It will be cathartic as well, allowing you to let go of negative feelings and to keep them in the past locked.

How and why does counseling succeed in "controlling" emotions?

Therapy provides a safe, supportive environment in which to build emotional intelligence by gazing compassionately and critically at your own thoughts and feelings and relational past.

Thinking about the causes and emotional states maintainers helps you clarify the role that they play in both positive and negative life circumstances.

Recognizing and exploring contradictory emotions often contributes to reducing anxiety and unblocking energy bound by indecision and releasing it for action.

Learning that attitudes change over time and understanding how, why and what is acceptable at the moment will minimize shame.

Feeling and showing emotions properly can help reduce depression if it is triggered by a need to control and prevent rage, jealousy, remorse or some other negative emotion.

CHAPTER 6

Emotional Influencer

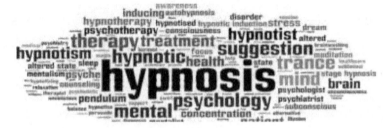

It is a power that until this point you're probably unaware of. The secret power you have to control your emotions, and influence them. How do we shape our emotions? It's a conditioned responses with a known method. So this is how it works:

"You're attending a public speaking event, waiting for it to begin. You and the rest of the audience members start applauding as soon as the speaker walks out on stage. The speaker is thankful to the audience, and continues on to speak. They exit the stage when they're done, and a few minutes later the next speaker walks on stage. Once again, you and the other members of the audience continue to cheer, and the speaker again kindly thanks the crowd.'

This situation is normal, and occurs so much that we no longer recognize it. Public speaking meetings, lectures, festivals, shows, when the host comes out on stage, the crowd claps, and after they applaud, the speaker says thank you. We are doing this without someone asking us directly why we need to. We immediately clap, and the speaker or presenter in exchange will say thanks to the audience, immediately. So it looks like a programmed reaction. It is a reaction to a given stimuli or signal. The cause or signal in the above case will be the speaker coming out on the stage and signaling that it's the cue to clap in.

There are some programmed reactions everywhere we go. In traffic, someone cuts you off, you immediately feel irritated. You arrive at work to see the pile of papers under which you need to go; you feel overwhelmed. You see a member of your loved one or kin, your face lights up automatically with a grin and you feel content. You step down the street past a series of shops and cafes, a certain scent wafts by and catches your nose and you are pulled back into your childhood instantly. It's a cue response method, but what you definitely didn't know is that you can enable these cue answer systems to function for you.

How do you control your emotions?

A repetitive response is a tendentious response to replicate itself. Let's imagine a buddy came along and invited you to go with them and get a cup of coffee. You might say yes or you could say no, based on what's going on at the moment. If that friend were to ask you 10 minutes later the same question, the reaction could be different then. Maybe you said no earlier, but 10 minutes later the response could be yes. This is not a programmed reaction since it is not repetitive or repeatable. Now, on the other side, anyone frightened of spiders is giving a predictable response. They go into panic mode as soon as they see a spider (the warning or stimulus) or start flipping out every single time. That's a predictable response; in this instance, the spider triggers the predictable response of fear.

Any cue which provokes a predictable answer is like an anchor. Anchoring is a very powerful procedure known as Neuro-Linguistic Programming (NLP) and is widely employed. Anchoring is better defined as a neural correlation, much like a conditioned reaction, between a tone, scenario or circumstance and the action that we have when we come face to face with that case. Anchoring lets one convey a desirable constructive emotional reaction when confronted with a certain sensation. You could wear a piece of apparel you call "the lucky hat," or a charm bracelet for good luck, maybe even a lucky pair of socks. These factors are all signs that cause a certain reaction or feeling inside you. You see, you already know at some stage that you can activate certain replies. Case after event, wearing fortunate clothing products. This ensures that if you have the right cue, you can get whatever answer you want in yourself, or anyone else. We learn from feelings as well as actual experiences. And, all of these components decide how we treat ourselves. While not necessarily straightforward it is important to observe certain behavior.

In 1927 Ivan Pavlov coined the term Classical Conditioning, and his method is still used as a point of reference to this day because of how simply it indicates learned behavior at work. Pavlov claimed action could be taught through conditioning where a stimulus is issued, and a reaction responds. His most famous experiment on this principle was when, in expectation of food, he trained dogs to begin salivating at the sound of the bell. The food served as a conditioned stimulation, and the reaction was salivation. Classical training is nowadays a well-recognized method in fundamental learning.

Another form of conditioning that is sometimes referred to as instrumental conditioning is operational conditioning. This procedure was studied by B.F. Skinner, who insisted that tapping at individual impulses to understand or regulate actions was futile. The behavior here is dictated by the results of an intervention, which could be in the context of incentive or penalty. Skinner claimed that acts that generate positive consequences appear to replicate themselves, while activities that contribute to retribution are unlikely to reproduce themselves. Strong improvement in this way would facilitate potential replication of the behavior. Activity is regulated by factors present while activity is promoted or penalized.

What these teach us is that there are different stimuli and responses you may build and configure. You have the ability to do so and this works for two reasons:

Pattern Recognition-This implies that the subconscious will learn from past encounters and adapt which learned behavior to new situations and the like. The pattern detection effectively stops you from committing the same error again. There's an evolutionary explanation why the brain is built for pattern recognition dependent function. As our early ancestors faced a vicious intruder and barely escaped with their life, the brain begins to recognize why they extend their learned knowledge the next time they encounter anything unfamiliar and remember they can run before the attacker strikes. This also appears to be how the shaping and anchoring work. You enter a particular situation and that situation triggers a specific cue which then elicits a particular response. If the condition plays well (positive or bad experience) depends.

Action Energy-Dr. David Hamilton, who has had a group of people performing a simple song on the piano over the span of many weeks, performed research on this topic. When he was confident the music was cemented in the brains of the people, he took a brain scan while they performed the album. He then took another brain scan, this time telling participants to visualize performing the song only by themselves. Examining the findings of all side by side brain scans, there was no way to determine which brain scan was different. This means that to our brain, there is no difference between having the actual experience or vividly imagine it. This argument stresses that building anchors for oneself is still quite important.

How Your Thoughts Can Influence Your Emotions

We need to go back to NLP to understand how our thoughts can influence our emotions. The expression "NLP" refers to the mind language. Neuro is the reference brain component whereas linguistic is the language section. Simply put, NLP is about learning your brain's language (mental). It is hard to forge a link when we don't understand the language our subconscious talks. So it often seems like you don't have power of your thoughts or emotions. Because it lacks the vital connection. It's like being out in a foreign country on holidays. You are in unfamiliar territory where no one has spoken your tongue, you cannot understand it and they cannot understand you. How does that feel? Most of the time stressful, because you are constantly struggling to get yourself heard.

NLP has a lot to do with the wisdom of the feelings. It shows you how to communicate through your mind's language, how to perceive your mind and how someone else could think. It helps you to connect consciously with your subconscious mind to understand better what you want out of life. Your subconscious mind is a powerful thing, and when you are able to tap that power to harness it to improve your life for the better, there's no indication what kind of success you can achieve. NLP teaches you how to get in tune with your mind, so that you can understand it in a way that you never had before. This allows you to become more emotionally intelligent and thus learn to be in control of your emotions and manipulate them.

By using NLP and emotional intelligence, you develop the ability to constructively and objectively perceive, utilize, and manage emotions. It allows you better equipped to understand other people's emotional condition and effectively engage with them in a manner that is mutually beneficial, supportive and trustworthy to all. By understanding the language of the mind and integrating it with emotional intelligence, you will encourage relationship development, build authentic relationships and create meaningful interactions, particularly with the groups of people that we find most challenging to communicate with such as friends, supervisors, team members, clients and more.

The following steps are required to master your emotions and allow your thoughts to influence the way you wish to feel:

Reframe the Material-This technique is extremely helpful if we feel helpless or weighing down negative thoughts and emotions. Reframing involves taking up a negative circumstance and strengthening oneself by changing the meaning with which you equate the experience, making it into a positive experience afterwards. It starts by identifying the negative scenario, like, for example, divorce. Divorce is never convenient, but let's just reframe it. What are the positive results of getting divorced? Now you can switch to other partnerships.

As you have learned valuable lessons, you can also look forward to forming a better relationship with the next person. You have the opportunity to do the stuff you couldn't do while you are in the relationship before. You took, then reframed, a pessimistic situation to make yourself a completely different experience.

Shifting the attention to more optimistic things only makes you feel easier, so you can make informed choices.

Sub modalities Producing-NLP sub modalities are categorized as visual, sensory, kinesthetic, and olfactory / gustative. -- Sub modality reflects the way our interactions are encoded and assigned significance. The NLP assumes the subjective meaning of the brain codes differently. This implies that the brain of everyone can code differently, depending on their own mental "picture" or portrayal. Sub modalities are among the NLP strategies that can either implicitly or explicitly help you relieve the tension. Using sub modalities can help you understand how to disassociate yourself from tension, so your actions doesn't show it. Listening to the way you behave is the first step in changing the sub modalities. When you have an unusually intense or stressed feeling, try something constructive that prevents your mind from dwelling on the bad.

You need NLP to help you communicate with your subconscious and appreciate your feelings in a way that you never before have been able to. What you think and believe is going to be two separate items, just something you want to say. The NLP is supposed to fill the distance between the subconscious and conscious mind. It's about starting to learn what the subconscious is trying to teach you. Without that awareness, relating yourself to your emotions would be difficult, which would then make it harder for you to control your actions and body language. To learn how to regulate your emotions you need to be able to identify and break through your current limitations. The aim of the NLP is to learn how to reach into the subconscious mind to become more likely to control the emotions.

Also, mental structures compose of details and know-how groups. Such details contain common words, personalities, processes, perceptions, informal myths, and opinions of the environment. Mental structures structure information in such a manner that it is understood, clarified and utilized. Mental models integrate knowledge and allow us to organize complex information into simpler concepts.

A wide base of visual templates strengthens our analytical abilities and encourages positive decision taking, the development of concepts and expertise for problem-solving. The consistency of our reasoning is directly related to the templates open to us and how we implement such templates in daily contexts.

We continue to create blind holes in our reasoning and decision-making method because we don't have adequate visual templates to guide our thoughts and decisions. Such blind points are our Achilles heel as the devil is in the specifics, ad another cliché goes. Getting blind spots in the process of thinking ensures that you can miss important aspects of a situation and as such the decision you are taking will be misinformed.

Creating a latticework of theoretical constructs to make the decision-making smoother should be a constant cycle of learning and creating multiple schools of thinking. The more insight we acquire and know the more our conceptual models grow. To really profit from behavioral templates, we need to be able to put aside old ways of thought to accept new insights.

New insights expand our perception and offer us a multi-dimensional viewpoint that reaches beyond our own beliefs. Those are some of the visual templates we should use to make informed decisions;

How the body affects emotions

An explosion of laughter as a funny event occurs. In moments of sorrow the eyes flowing down the cheeks. A line rising on the forehead. The surge of discomfort in your stomach in reaction to the anxious butterflies. A jolt of anticipation as you open a package. One thing is for sure; our feelings elicit a physical reaction very strongly. The fast pulses of feeling in the spur of the moment that we experience in our bodies are just a tiny example of how feelings literally affect us. Yeah, how strong is the relationship between mind and body? Does one impact the other? How much, if so?

There are several forms the human body reacts to our emotional health. Let's look at an example of what could happen if our mental health isn't doing too well. The pH levels of the body start fluctuating when you're anxious, nervous, concerned or sad. This is responsible for the associated observed stomach aches, constipation, nausea or high blood pressure. Your immunity system gets weakened when you are continually depressed or nervous. For e.g., when we experience anxiety, the heart rate and respiration rate of our body go into overdrive to encourage our brains to get more oxygen. This lets us react to any complex scenario in an effective manner. Our immune system gets a quick boost when this occurs, and then when the tension passes our body naturally operates at the right rate again. But becoming continuously anxious and stressed means the body is continually overdriving and it never gets the chance to return to normal functioning. As a consequence, our immune system continues to erode, leaving us more vulnerable to infectious illnesses, viruses and more frequently we get sick too. If you ask why during especially stressful times you seem to fall sick even faster, that's why.

You're much more likely to overlook your physical health when you're feeling moody or stressed too because it's going to be the last thing on your mind. Instead, you 're going to yield to the unpleasant temptations that are increasingly starting to become more challenging to ignore and you're heading for the fatty treats or the bottle of wine the you realize you shouldn't.

Other ways our emotions influence our body include:

Affecting the cardiovascular function-Our pulse rhythm starts to quicken as we undergo an anxiety attack, pounding vigorously against the abdomen. This raises heart rate, which is why people suffering from anxiety or panic disorder frequently experience heart palpitations and chest pressure, mistaking it for an incident of cardiac disease at times. If you still have heart failure, fear from become overly depressed, this issue is compounded and the likelihood of cardiovascular complications is raised further.

Affecting the cardiovascular system-The heavy breathing encountered as fear kicks in causes it harder to breathe, and if you also have untreated obstructive pulmonary disease, then you are at a higher risk of symptoms due to anxiety. For those struggling with asthma, anxiety, and living in a constant condition of heightened stressed feelings, the symptoms of asthma that you have can become worse.

Affecting the Central Nervous System of the Body: Long-term tension and anxiety constantly trigger our brains to produce stress hormones as a method for coping. The body often begins to develop headaches as this occurs, and sometimes feels dizziness. Eventually this persistent condition of perpetuity contributes to depression. When a human begins to feel stressed and anxious, their nervous system is filled with chemicals and hormones that are designed to respond to this danger, namely adrenaline and cortisol. Although this is good when you really go to an extremely traumatic experience, long-term stress hormone use may be very dangerous. Long-term cortisol exposure may contribute to weight gain, too.

Affecting the digestive system-Feeling intense emotional waves might theoretically impact your digestive system too, particularly if fear is what you're struggling with. Emotions may induce aches in the stomach, diarrhea, nausea and lack of appetite. Irritable intestinal syndrome (IBS) and bowel disorders related to excessive or lack of bowel movements may be another possible side effect based on how much the feelings influence you. In addition, IBS induces diarrhea, vomiting and constipation. For having not so good symptoms.

It requires a lot of patience and commitment to try to keep a grip to your feelings. If it seems like you're using every ounce of energy that you've left to regulate your feelings, it will leave you feeling exhausted, lonely, lonely, tired and physically sore. Although emotions are a part of who we are, our bodies have not been engineered for long periods to accommodate adrenalin and cortisol. Adrenaline leaves you sweating, jumpy and incapable of sleeping, often so paralyzed in terror you can no longer respond. To make it worse, coping with the exhaustion that accompanies these exhausting times makes it hard to get the required restful night sleep you deserve. Being sleep-deprived also makes it more difficult to stay in control. But maybe the greatest side-effect of all is the risk that while you fail to contain and manage your feelings, you bring your heart inside.

Yet not just negative news. As well as feelings may have a detrimental effect on you, they are able to do the reverse, too. For example; when you feel happier, your breathing and heart rate is increasing. The brain produces more endorphins and dopamine, the chemical pleasure which our bodies need to feel positive about. There was also a thinking about becoming comfortable and happy to stimulate the development about fresh brain cells, which in turn tends to enhance our cognitive ability and memory.

Emotions have a large part to play in our physical wellbeing. Having to pay attention to these signals may be effective in signaling that our mental wellbeing may not get anything quite right. Through listening to your body, you will start taking the appropriate steps to better affect your health and enhance your physical and mental wellness in the process. The explanation we end up being depressed and nervous and finding it impossible to get out of this toxic loop is that we do not give adequate value to wellness of mind, body and spirit. Taking control of our bodies involves not just the physical dimensions but also the social and emotional dimensions. Too often, we are so centered on the physical aspect that we ignore and overlook that there is an entirely different element that also requires attention and care. We don't know the degree to which tension, concern and anxiety will weigh down on us.

The perfect way to learn how to control your emotions, and use them to affect the body positively? Measurement. Consistent meditation disables the distractions that we face by filtering it out before bottleneck begins. It's like a barrier in the river that means the correct amount of water moves and meets where it wants to go. In the same way, meditation filters the less important data to which we are exposed, and sends only the necessary and important information into our brain. In other words, it helps us to determine what information we should focus on, and what we need not focus on can cause chronic anxiety. A 2005 study by Dr. Sara Lazar was a groundbreaking study showing the brains of those who were meditating were much smoother and had more folds and surface area in their prefrontal cortexes. This study is now used as the go-to foundational study for other mental health issues such as depression by various neuroscientific and psychological researches. Those who meditate normally are anxiety-free, happy, and healthy, even for 10 to 15 minutes a day.

Harvard psychiatrist Herbert Benson sometime in the 1970s looked at the actions of the patients who visited him because of their stress-related disorders. His observation led him to look into ways he could overcome this connection, revolutionizing the mental care sector in the process at the same time. Dr. Benson's discovery was the relation, by meditation, between mind and body. It reduced metabolism, lowered heart rate, gave rise to regulated breathing and quieter brainwave function. All of this together has provided the right basis for recovery. Our body activates the parasympathetic nervous system while meditating, and deactivates the tension state of the body at the same time. When this happens, the body reverses a number of health issues, especially fear, which supports research by Dr. Benson. The link between mind and body puts the body in the meditative state it requires to relieve anxiety, manage stress, and balance the strong, overwhelming emotions we are all battling at some point.

Why Words affect your emotions

Being overly emotional may cause behavioral variations. You become inclined to act and communicate in a manner you wouldn't usually do. Once something is said and done, it's all there is for it. It can never be reversed, and one can never forget the words that have been said. This is why you need to work hard every day to maintain control over one of the most powerful forces that is occurring inside you. The ability to know, understand , and respond to emotions correctly, overcome stress, and be mindful of our words and actions, and how they influence others, is how we can become effective in learning to control our emotions.

The vocabulary we use most often determines the basic capabilities of our brain and the unconscious processes that we are exposed to because of that language. Being mindful of how we use our language is therefore one of the most important factors that will determine the condition of our emotional wellness. To put it another way, if you want to be content you need to use the best words and language. We depend on language to describe the various sensations, events and experiences that we are experiencing. We use words to give a name on the feeling we experience at the moment. The multiple terms we use generate contrasting physiological responses. Two individuals may be going through the same scenario for example. Person A says, "That's good, things might have been worse," when Person B responds, "This is the worst thing that might ever have happened to me." Person A would be the one with a healthier, somewhat satisfied mental well-being merely through choosing different phrases to express the same circumstance.

Words can be a strong force of good when used for the right reasons but it can be used to cause great harm and suffering on the other end of the spectrum. The pen is more effective than the sword comes from the very real fact that words may inflict more damage and leave scars so deep they may never recover fully. Once the English philosopher and writer Aldous Huxley said that words were like an X-ray. These terms, when used in derogatory ways, will reach into almost anything. Dignity, self-esteem, the right kind of terms may also challenge another's personality.

To continue to use words in a way that has a more positive effect on our mental well-being, we need to begin to change our vocabulary to show appreciation. Respect for our feelings, and appreciation for the circumstances that push us through those interactions to become a better person. We need to rephrase the vocabulary that we use so that we accept our feelings for what they are rather than attempting to deny their existence. Instead of treating them like an enemy we need to use our words to understand our negative emotions. Metaphors can be potent tools in this situation. They are often used to help convey and emphasize messages in books, movies, and commercials. They have the same potent effect that positive assertions have. To build a healthy mindset shift involves that you use only meaningful terms and definitions, and choose the ones that work best for you.

To start developing a new way of thinking, you need to start utilizing terms that encourage positivity while saying them. Positive, optimistic words, full of potential, love, joy, happiness and success. Those words will ultimately reflect your existence. The mind hears exactly what you say, and believes what you say so long as you have no doubt about yourself. Do not try to copy the metaphors of someone else, because it has to be something that resonates deeply with you. It has to be something with which you feel connected, something that stirs up powerful emotions and drive the motivation to be better. The metaphors of somebody else may work well for them, but this may not necessarily work for you as well, because your priorities would be different. It is important that you hear yourself using the right words. Think of how you have represented your life up to now, for example. What kind of vocabulary are you applying? Are words that come to mind like boring, tired, depressed, or worried first thought? Negative words may become a prophecy which fulfills itself.

Image your very own dream. Visualize it as though it was really occurring and you are the guy you want to be. What are you watching? Will you be pleased with the character characteristics you see, if you had to look at yourself from the lens of another person? Be crystal-clear about the vision and that will help you define the terms you need to use to identify yourself in this perfect form. Be resolved to never ever identify yourself with those harsh descriptive terms. Now that you realize the words are more important than you could have blamed them with originally, here's what you should do to make sure you use the correct kind of words the positively affect your emotions:

Reflect on keeping your philosophy optimistic-Concentrate on keeping your default mode productive, and inspire everyone to do the same. If your subconscious will lament and be pessimistic without ever worrying about it, so you should probably start managing your emotions in order to do the reverse. You ought to pretend you are a motivational speaker to do as they do-advise to educate-to become a more diligent person with an positive outlook on life. Speak for positivity at every reasonable chance. It is a consistency which is infectious. So, not only will you be inspiring yourself, but you will also be motivating others to be more optimistic. Plus, the habit of using positive dialogue, the most you say them, can reaffirm the terms of your vocabulary.

Take a Cue from books-Much enjoyed by successful people. Therefore they are in absolute possession of their emotions, bringing into their world exactly what they want. Now you are approaching the early stages of learning to be in the driver's seat to be the one in charge of your mind rather than offering it that same force.

The most crucial ones are those early stages. It's when the mind starts to relearn, to regrow. A regeneration, to put it that way. You need to feed it with the nourishment that comes in the form of encouraging books, to help it grow. Devour constantly, daily. Take note of the vocabulary used in these books and aim to use the same kind of language in your everyday life. The more motivational they get, the stronger. Any book that strengthens your commitment, self-discipline and stamina. Store up on books that motivate and inspire you to make your dreams come true. Load them in with your books.

Be an Edison-that is to say, Thomas Edison. Thomas Edison couldn't have said it better when he said, I'm paraphrasing, I didn't fail, I only discovered 1000 forms of not having a light bulb. After all, if Edison had let it deter him, today we would not be celebrating his amazing achievements. See how the terms he used altered his perception? He actually interpreted what everyone else had seen as a disappointment as an opportunity to learn. Likewise our errors can provide great moments of instruction. This easy way to control your emotions and the phrases that you are using will make a big difference.

Developing a motivational environment is tantamount to creating a conducive environment that promotes positivity through pictures of motivational quotes, sayings, mantras or room objectives. Anything that moves you is a nice addition to that. Print bright, vivid signs, and word or photo art that encourages you. Choose photos that inspire you to concentrate on your current task and to carry through. Write motivational quotes on post-it notes if you are working in a cubicle, and place it around your office.

CONCLUSION

The definition of emotional intelligence is mind-blowing, but what is so cool about it is that you may have earned the lowest score on the exam today so you will do the test again in a few months' lessons to earn the maximum score. It is assumed an improved level of emotional intelligence is a predictor of success. You should grow to be emotionally wise no matter who you are or where you are in the structure of the office or the organizations with which you operate.

There are many success stories recorded by people who have attained any level of emotional intelligence; several success stories describe cases of body healing, telepathy, intellectual intelligence, and much more. However, it is very important for an individual to obtain professional assistance before implementing any kind of high mental attention, any behavior or thoughts in these aspects may actually cause mental strain that may not be good especially for those with a long streak of mental illness. It is stated that the simple acts required to have a high emotional quotient are behaviors such as positive thinking on a given situation.

Emotional intelligence can never happen overnight, it takes some time for this act to be fully incorporated into a human system of thinking. Knowing the process of attraction rules and other world rules may be very complicated as truly understanding the states of mind. However, preparation and persistence produce certain subconscious learning of a certain path of emotional intelligence, the learning of the subconscious mind is the guiding force behind the performance in emotional intelligence.

It is important to have positive behavior knowledge that you may want to influence brain exercise when it comes to having knowledge about it, particularly it can be scooped from a variety of websites that show information about it. It's pretty easy to locate these websites; all you need to do is type the term 'emotional intelligence' into your preferred web search engine to navigate such pages. It's suggested to get details from places that show impartial topic material. Emotional intelligence will open the path to immerse progress in life.

Emotional intelligence is about integrating inner and outer existence. So long as our desire to control our objectives interferes with all strategies, we will profit from our EQ. A counterbalance between personal and social aspects is taking us back to EQ's full value.

One of the critical steps to becoming a brilliant leader is managing the feelings. You will do this through the application of the lessons in this book's chapters. Concentrate on the emotional intelligence 5 tools to leverage to lead well.

Know How to listen and communicate

You've also realized how often your mind is more occupied planning what you're going to answer when you're talked to than genuinely actively listening to it. At all times, you must escape this pit, and not only understand the content of what you are being told, but also infer the feelings and emotions behind the words spoken. Usually more important than what's said is what sits behind the words. As a boss you can at least fulfill the need to be respected if you can't answer all the complaints. You'll gain the opportunity to "talk" with others and stay informed about what's going on.

Understand and Filter Your Emotions

The foundation of any emotional intelligence is your emotional awareness, what triggers them and how you react. The more you are aware of what's happening, the more you are able to develop skills that will help you handle them well and adapt to any stressful or unpleasant circumstance appropriately and effectively. You must be able to think on what may be the best decision, instead of reacting quickly. If you respond without analyzing your emotions, you risk penalizing your partnerships and stirring up mistrust in your community.

Take heed and move before it's too late

With these skills to feel towards people, situations and moods, you must be able to anticipate how people are likely to react to a particular situation, and thus intervene before it is too late. Preparing for bad news events such as a layoff or closing allows you to better handle the situation with the people involved when it happens. Rather than leaving the field exposed to the crippling gossip, it's easier to hold the land and leverage the emotional and social skills to assist them through those moments.

Feel and Decipher the Emotions of Others

It's good to be aware of your feelings, but you must also be aware of the emotions expressed by others, what triggered them, examine them and appreciate them.

Understand without getting through their game to the extent that they sink in it and are consumed by it. It is not a matter of going immediately to a conclusion of your conversation or making a rash decision, but rather of finding, analyzing and understanding the origins of your interlocutor's emotional reaction.

Take the Pulse of the Morale of the Troops

To be an effective leader, you not only need to be aware of what's happening but also know how to catch the entire team's mood, worries and dreams. The morale of the troops is affected by several factors: the risk of losing his job, a colleague's departure, the gossip regarding the company's financial problems, duty conflicts, and competitors' envy that directly impacts the emotional wellbeing. If your staff knows that you care for and are looking for solutions, trust, loyalty and success, they can owe you and their work and performance standards the same respect.

CPSIA information can be obtained
at www.ICGtesting.com
Printed in the USA
BVHW090841230421
605637BV00001B/138